D1039586

# Beyond Belief

A True Story of Ultimate Forgiveness

# Ray H. Richardson

*Beyond Belief*

*Beyond Belief*

A True Story of Ultimate Forgiveness

**Ray H. Richardson**

Mary Johnson with photo of son, Laramiun Byrd.

# ACKNOWLEDGMENTS

**June Richardson-Chavez, mother of 'Beyond Belief' author and my everlasting inspiration!**

## Visitation Sisters of Minneapolis

Sister Mary Margaret McKenzie

Sister Mary Frances Reis

Sister Suzanne Homeyer

Sister Mary Virginia Schmidt

Sister Karen Mohan

Sister Katherine Mullin

Sister Brenda Lisenby

Mary Johnson

Oshea Israel

Dave Nimmer, advisor

## Minnesota Department of Corrections

Bruce Reiser, Deputy Commissioner

Tim Hansen, former Minnesota DOC restorative justice planner

Regina Stepney, former Program Coordinator for Stillwater Correctional Facility

Sherlinda Wheeler, Program Coordinator for Oak Park Correctional Facility

Patrick Courtney, Records and Data

**Victim-Offender Dialogues In Crimes Of Severe Violence - June 2007**

Collaboration study by the University of Minnesota and Minnesota DOC

Hennepin County District Court Records

Hennepin County Coroner's Office

North Regional Library, Minneapolis

Sumner Library, Minneapolis

Kimberly 'Glam Life Kim' Holifield

Tooties Restaurant, Minneapolis

*'Total Forgiveness'* by R.T. Kendall, Charisma House, 2002

Michele Braley, former Minnesota DOC facilitator

Brian Mogren, St. Jane House

Regina Irwin, Mary Johnson's close friend

Annette Dillard, Mary Johnson's close friend

Ed Roy, Mary's husband

Thomas Kelly, Visitation Sisters legal counsel

John McShane, former Hennepin County District Judge

'Two Mothers' poem (Author unknown)

Priscilla Scott and Regina Ann Smith — Mary

Johnson's Two Mothers organization

    Carolyn Green, Oshea's mother

    Rev. John Ortberg, Menlo Park (Calif.) Presbyterian Church

    CBS Evening News

    People Magazine

    'The View' TV show

    Conference of Fair Sentencing for Youth; Washington, D.C.

**"Forgiveness is the attribute of the strong."**

*Mahatma Gandhi (1869-1948)*

# FOREWORD

## By Dave Nimmer

Beyond Belief is the result of a spiritual partnership between a white nun who sought to explore the privilege from the color of her skin and a black mother who wanted relief from the resentment toward the man who killed her son.

At Sister Mary Margaret McKenzie's request, her Visitation community of North Minneapolis commissioned this book about Mary Johnson-Roy and her journey toward forgiving Oshea Israel, who murdered her 20-year-old son, Laramiun Byrd, Feb. 12, 1993.

When the two first met, Johnson-Roy was grieving the loss of her son and working to form a group of mothers who also lost children to violence. The two "Marys" became fast friends. They share a belief in a loving God, who forgives the sins of His children and asks that they "forgive those who trespass against" them.

Over the past decade, the two women have prayed together, traveled together, and worked together to promote and define the grace of forgiveness. Mary Johnson-Roy has a message for those who read Beyond Belief:

"I want them to know what forgiveness is. I want them to know what freedom is. I need to be forgiven and I need to forgive. The grace of forgiveness leads to a more gentle and hopeful world. We can get unstuck and move on — and do what we should do for the rest of our lives."

Mary Johnson-Roy and Mary Margaret McKenzie provide a gracious example for all of us. Shed resentments. Accept responsibility. Seek reconciliation. And in this way, be who you are and be that well.

*Dave Nimmer is a retired reporter who worked at WCCO-TV and the Minneapolis-Star Tribune.*

# INTRODUCTION
## By Ray H. Richardson

*Could you do it?*

It's a strong probability that you know someone who has lost a family member or friend to a violent crime.

Let's get personal. That individual could be you. You could be in the ever-growing category of individuals suffering the loss of a family member or friend to violence. If you have, my condolences to you.

How do you feel about that incident today? Do you want revenge? Has the justice system taken care of it? Or are you hoping that some type of divine intervention takes out the perpetrator?

These are just some of the instinctive reactions people around the world experience when a criminal act takes the life of someone close to them. Over time, the immediate pain subsides and occasionally forgiveness takes over to help people move on with their lives.

Let's get personal again. One of my childhood friends in Chicago was beaten to death in 2018 by his son in their home. Carl's son had mental problems that tragically exploded one day. I was among many kids on our block on Chicago's South Side who regularly congregated at Carl's house to listen to music in his driveway or set up our football or baseball games down the street. Carl was still living in the house after his parents died. It hurts knowing he's not there anymore. Even though my friend's son was unstable, I don't know if I could ever forgive him for taking away a part of my childhood.

Forgiveness! What an interesting word. What an interesting phenomenon. For some people, it's impossible and intolerable to consider forgiving someone who inflicted so much pain and heartbreak. That's why the immediate thought is revenge, harsh justice or the hope that "God will deal with them."

Making peace with someone who did you wrong is a very difficult move, yet we are taught at an early age about specific references in The Bible that address this dilemma: "In order for God to forgive your sins, you yourself must forgive…"

As much as we treasure the teachings of The Bible, the mere thought of forgiveness generates a raging conflict within us. It's the last thing on our minds when someone close is taken from us by a violent act. How do you change your feelings from hatred to compassion? How do you get to that seemingly unreachable place when you're no longer able to hug a loved one because somebody took their life? For those strong enough to do it, forgiveness is reached in numerous ways – counseling, going to church, emotional conversations with family or friends, public tributes, mediation, etc.

When people manage to get to the mountaintop and proclaim forgiveness towards someone, they feel whole as individuals, spiritually complete. In many ways, there's a rebirth of their soul and personality – all because they were able to throw away their grudges and hostilities. Raise your hand if you have experienced that feeling!

Understandably, there are some folks, maybe even yourself, who are keeping their hands down because they have yet to come face-to-face with a divine moment that motivates them to forgive. And these folks, according to Bible passages and beliefs, will continue to carry the weight of misery until they figure out this thing called forgiveness.

It is said that a person is not truly free from the hurt that was delivered to them until they forgive. Yes, it sounds impractical, and even unthinkable, but there is power in this premise.

There's a lady named Mary Johnson in Minneapolis who took the power of forgiveness beyond all heights imaginable. In the aftermath of losing her only child in a fatal shooting, and the shooting was not an accident, Mary has given us a lesson we all need to examine.

Could you do it? Could you do what Mary did to make herself whole as a person, to live righteously in the eyes of God? Remember these questions as you follow Mary's story. Along the way, continue to ask yourself, 'Could I do this'? Do I have it in me to do what Mary did? Is my faith strong enough to let God take me to that rare level of reconciliation? Even if you're not a deeply religious person, you have to ask yourself: 'Is there something inside that will allow me to pardon the criminal who tore apart my life.'

Your answers will have you thinking that this story really is Beyond Belief!

Laramiun at age 6.

# CHAPTER ONE

*Can't wait for Bible study class!*
*January 1993*

Mary Johnson has been on her phone at work so much this afternoon that she doesn't realize it's almost time to go home. It's Wednesday. Two community events she's coordinating for US West in Minneapolis are coming up this weekend and she's trying to finalize details.

When Mary is not processing orders for 1-800 numbers, her main function at the phone carrier corporation, she heads up her employer's North Side Community Service Team. Mary volunteered for the role to help her escape the boredom of filing those 1-800 orders all day. It's also a fun opportunity to get out of the company's downtown Minneapolis office on certain days. Mary enjoys her work with the community service team. She believes in US West's push to have a presence in the community, particularly on Minneapolis' North Side, the primary target area for the company's outreach efforts. The North Side houses a significant percentage of the African-Americans living in Minneapolis.

Mary has the responsibility of making sure she and her team have the necessary promotional materials and support equipment for events. The job often has satisfying results. There have been times when she and her team packed Thanksgiving bags with food and other items for families in need and people in homeless shelters. Under Mary's watch, US West has become a regular participant in National Night Out, an outdoor event in communities around the country designed to raise awareness on unity and crime prevention.

Mary's unit works on the eighth floor of US West's headquarters. Other smaller departments share the bustling space. The underlying chatter of phone conversations is a constant hum throughout the office. On a clear day, she can walk over to one of the huge office windows and get a glimpse of the nearby Mississippi River. The river, only a few blocks from the office, runs through downtown Minneapolis and provides a wonderful backdrop for daydreaming or meditating. In the summer months, employees take advantage of the balmy weather and have lunch by the river.

While on the phone talking to a staff member at a local community organization, Mary looks up at the clock and grimaces. It's 4:25. In five minutes, the office will shut down and folks will be heading to the elevators. Her desk is a mess and she's running out of time to wrap up items on her checklist. It looks like some of those items will have to wait until tomorrow. Mary does what she can to tidy up her work space. A Bible propped up on her desk gets special attention. She picks it up and gives it a gentle shake before placing it in her purse.

"Lord, thank you for getting me through this one," Mary says. "These folks have been working me today!"

Mary is glad to see this particular work day come to an end. Every Wednesday night is Bible study at her church, and Mary is a faithful participant. Unless Mary is sick or has to deal with a family emergency, she doesn't miss Bible study – and she's pretty good at ignoring temptation. Two female co-workers stop by Mary's desk on their way to the elevator to tell Mary they're going to a nearby bar for happy hour. They invite Mary to join them.

"Now, you know what day it is," Mary says smiling. "It's Wednesday. I'm going home. Then I'm going to church. Ya'll want to come with me?"

"I go to church on Sundays," one of the co-workers tells Mary. "The other days belong to me."

Mary fires back with a grin, "Are you sure about that?"

"All I know is I need to have a cocktail after being in this place today," her co-worker says.

The second co-worker agrees, "I heard that!"

They say goodbye to Mary and head to the elevator. Mary, however, gets the last word, "I'll pray for ya'll!"

Before leaving her desk, Mary glances at a notepad to make a final check of her agenda for tomorrow. She sets the notepad down and proceeds to the elevator, feeling good about her decision to not join her co-workers. At 40, Mary has learned the importance of relying on her faith and belief in God to maintain a happy spirit. Mary's mother, Ester, is in a nursing home; her father, Otis, is living with her so she can take better care of him.

Mary and her second husband, Randy, are separated. His drinking had become a growing concern for Mary. He eventually moved out and never returned, leaving her with most of the burden of caring for her parents. Randy was a big help to Mary. He would cook for Mary's parents and take her father to the nursing home every day to visit her mother.

The occasional stress on Mary's personal life doesn't end there. Her 20 year-old son, Laramiun, has been a sporadic resident in her home, moving in and out at his leisure. At the moment, he's living in North Minneapolis with his aunt, Mary's sister, Mildred. Mary doesn't mind Laramiun's independence, but she's unhappy with his lifestyle. Mary's role with the community service team has given her more connections in the community and sometimes those connections relay unsettling reports about her son.

Mary often hears that Laramiun is 'too young to be making the kind of money he is making…' The troubling thing for Mary is that she knows Laramiun doesn't have a job. So, how is he making all this money? Mary has an idea, but she keeps her distance from the truth. After dropping out of high school, Laramiun spent time in a juvenile detention center and the Hennepin County (Minnesota) Work House for selling drugs and riding in a stolen car.

The reports Mary has been hearing on the streets about Laramiun brought her to the sad conclusion that he's selling again. She has talked to him numerous times about his activities. Her words, and her tears, have yet to make a difference. She's worried that he could land behind bars again.

When Laramiun was in the detention center, Mary didn't visit him. It was her way of trying to teach him a lesson. She told him in a phone conversation while he was in the detention center, "This is what can happen if you keep fooling around…" Mary's decision to not visit Laramiun briefly strained their relationship, but she still loved her son.

Mary had grown weary of Laramiun's behavior. He was expelled from junior high after coming to school with a pen knife. Mary tried to get him back in school, even to the point of hiring an attorney, but they lost the case. Mary made one more attempt to get Laramiun on the right track, enrolling him in an alternative school as a ninth-grader. Laramiun didn't finish out the year. He reached the conclusion that the streets were a better environment for him than a classroom. He never goes back to school.

Mary is no different than most parents when it comes to raising their kids. She knows she could have been a better parent. As a kid, Laramiun would go to church with her. When he was 11, he sang in the youth choir. At the time, Mary saw no warning signs that Laramiun might be heading down a troubling path. Things changed when Laramiun became a teen-ager. One day Laramiun told Mary he had to wear his hat a certain way, otherwise he would get beat up. Mary suspected then that her son might be putting himself in detrimental situations. She had more reasons for concern when she found out that Randy had been teaching Laramiun how to shoot a gun. Randy and Laramiun remained close after Randy left Mary.

The fact that Laramiun was in and out of Mary's house as a kid, led to gaps in their relationship. Mary and Laramiun's father, Charles, Mary's first husband, were married for only a year. Charles and Laramiun remained close after the divorce. At nine years-old, Laramiun asked Mary if he could live with his father. Mary consented but she had a feeling Laramiun would be back. In less than a year, Laramiun wanted to come home. He didn't feel comfortable being around his father and his girlfriend. Laramiun was always welcomed back home. He is Mary's only child and her love for her son never wavers.

Mary's commitment to her church is a valuable distraction to her issues with Laramiun.

She's very involved in church functions and makes herself available when needed. Besides the weekly Bible study class, Mary is a member of the praise and worship team. There are many weeks when Mary is at her church every day.

Mary has changed into casual clothes after coming home from work. She goes into the kitchen to warm up a light meal to eat something before heading to Bible study class. Her full schedule at work today didn't leave her time to take lunch. She has about a half-hour to eat. She's always on time for Bible study and has no intention of changing her routine tonight.

Mary is sitting at her dining room table eating and reading today's paper when Laramiun walks into the house. He still has a key.

Laramiun is drawn to the kitchen by the aroma of food. He heads over to Mary and gives her a quick kiss on the cheek. "Hey Momma, what's that you're eating?"

Mary has a question for him, "What are you doing with a key to my house? I thought I told you to leave your key here when you moved out."

Laramiun goes to Mary's refrigerator and looks inside to see if he can find something to snack on, ignoring Mary's question. He doesn't answer until he pulls out several items to make a sandwich and closes the refrigerator door. "Momma, I told you I made a copy of the key."

"I don't remember that," Mary says in a stern, but playful tone. "I want that key. You don't live here anymore."

Laramiun smiles at Mary's reminder of his living status. He shrugs off his mother's demand to return her key and proceeds to make a sandwich. He sits down at the table to join her.

Mary shakes her head in disappointment. "Boy, what am I gonna do with you?"

Laramiun smiles again and takes a bite of his sandwich. He does not respond to Mary's question, preferring to ease his hunger pains. Mary and Laramiun talk briefly about recent "news items" they have heard around the neighborhood.

The conversation leads Mary to a dreaded topic with her son – again. "You know, I really wish you would stop doing all that dirt in the streets," Mary pleads. "Something might happen to you one day out there."

"Momma, nothing's gonna happen to me…Besides, I make more money than you do."

Laramiun's claim that he makes more money than his mother draws a glare from Mary. "At least, I don't have to worry about somebody knocking me upside my head one day!" She really doesn't mind if Laramiun's income is better than hers, but it's the source of the income that bothers her. She can't help but worry that Laramiun might find himself in trouble again. She's had countless talks with Laramiun about his activities. The response is usually the same.

*"Momma, you don't have to worry about me. I'm good. I'm gonna get that boat I've been talking about, so I can do my fishing and just chill on the lake."*

"Yeah, right…I gotta go." Mary gets up to put her plate in the sink.

Laramiun asks Mary where she's going. Mary tells him she's going to Bible study class at church. Laramiun has another question. He asks Mary if she can do him a "favor."

The question makes Mary stop in her tracks in disbelief. "What kind of favor you want from me?" she asks with a stern look on her face.

Laramiun reaches into his jacket pocket and pulls out a white athletic sock that appears to be stuffed with something. He lays the sock on the table and takes another bite of his sandwich. "Will you keep this for me?"

"What is it? What's in that sock?"

"Just some money," Laramiun said before taking another bite. Mary glares at her son again. This time her look is more intense.

Laramiun can tell she is not happy.

Mary takes a closer look at the sock and sees a few dollar bills bulging out. The entire sock is filled with folded bills of various values.

If Laramiun emptied the sock, the money would cover a good portion of the table.

Mary has no interest in asking Laramiun how much money is in the sock. She knows the money came from the streets and she wants no part of it. "Put that sock back in your pocket and take it with you when you leave. I don't want you bringing that kind of money into my house. I'm not going to hold drug money for you."

She shakes her head in disgust as she puts on her coat and grabs her purse. She has a lot more to say to her son, but Bible study is starting in a few minutes. Any other night, she would be more than willing to have a fierce debate with her son in the kitchen to discuss his lifestyle. Laramiun is lucky it's Wednesday. In a rigid voice, Mary tells Laramiun, "We need to talk some more...Like I always do, I'm gonna pray for you."

Mary heads toward a side door in her kitchen to leave the house.

Laramiun gets up and walks over to Mary to give her a kiss on the cheek.

Mary just looks at Laramiun, then turns to go through the door.

"See you later Momma!"

Mary and Laramiun at age 8.

Until we have seen someone's darkness, we don't really know who they are. Until we have forgiven someone's darkness, we don't really know what love is.

Marianne Williamson

# CHAPTER TWO

## *Marlon's search for success*

*January 1993*

Another look of frustration is visible on Marlon Green's face as he stands outside an Old Country Buffet restaurant waiting for his mother, Carolyn, to pick him up and drive him to their Minneapolis apartment.

The number of job applications and interviews is beginning to wear on Marlon's patience. Each inquiry ends with a similar result – no openings or a generic goodbye.

*"Thanks for coming in! We'll call you in a couple of weeks. Good luck to you!"*

Marlon heard that expression again after his brief interview with a manager at Old Country Buffet. At 16 and not in school, Marlon is wondering if his job searching is worth the effort. Yesterday, he applied for work at a barber shop and the Minneapolis Park District. He spent the rest of the day looking through the yellow pages to get ideas on where he could go to find a job. Maybe Marlon could use a quick tutoring session in job search etiquette. He showed up at the restaurant wearing jeans and gym shoes. A T-shirt displaying a picture of rapper Scarface was visible underneath his heavy jacket.

Perceptions and decorum are not at the top of Marlon's agenda list. Five months earlier, he was kicked out of Minneapolis North High School for gang activity and fighting. As a member of the Gangster Disciples, he had developed a reputation around the school for being one of the street gang's leaders. His freshman year at North High lasted only a month.

With no previous employment experience and no apparent education plans, Marlon is dangerously close to a stereotype that scars many young African-American males. What's the future for teens like Marlon if they're not in school and not working? Society tends to have a chart line for African-American youths in that category – no education and no employment leads to jail, prison or death. Most teens like Marlon are too young or too preoccupied to analyze where they see themselves in five years. The priority is day-to-day survival and Marlon is in serious survival mode.

Marlon's disappointment from today's interview doesn't last long. While waiting outside for his mother to pick him up, a stylish black SUV slowly rolls by with music blaring from custom-made speakers. On this cold day in January, the car's windows are up but the volume on the speakers is loud enough for Marlon to hear the song, a tune by popular rapper 2Pac, one of Marlon's favorite artists.

The three African-American men in the car are bobbing their heads to the beat of the music.

Marlon bobs his head slightly as well. He has an envious look in his eyes as he watches the car continue down the street. "Life is good for somebody out here," Marlon mumbles.

Moments later, Carolyn pulls up in front of the restaurant. She doesn't make Marlon feel any better when he gets inside the car.

"Boy, what do you have on? How do you expect to get a job dressed like that?"

Marlon rolls his eyes. He forces a quick grin to hide his somber attitude after another failed job search. "Thanks for picking me up Mom," Marlon says with a trace of sarcasm.

Carolyn is not happy to see the way Marlon is dressed, but she flashes a forgiving smile as she drives off and offers her son some motherly comfort. She can tell by the look in his eyes that her son is still unemployed. "Don't you give up!" Carolyn tells him. "Keep following through! It'll happen! I just want you to keep trying, so you can stop whatever you're doing out here in these streets!"

When Marlon was 14, Carolyn found marijuana in his bedroom and put him on punishment for a month.

Marlon stays silent during his mother's words of encouragement, opting to look out the window at nothing in particular. He knows his mother is right. He's heard these words from her before, but despite not having a job, he's not broke. Selling drugs has kept money in his pocket when he needed it, and another deposit was about to happen.

When Carolyn and Marlon pull up to their apartment, Marlon sees two young men standing near their entrance. Marlon recognizes the men. They are customers waiting for his return.

Carolyn sees the men too. She wants to quiz Marlon about the men, but she doesn't have time. She's meeting up with friends for dinner in downtown Minneapolis.

Carolyn and Marlon exchange goodbyes before he gets out of the car.

Carolyn waves at him and drives off.

Marlon nods to the men as he walks toward the entrance to his apartment building. The men nod back to Marlon. He tells the men to wait for him outside near the building's parking lot. Marlon goes upstairs to his apartment to get a small plastic bag in his bedroom. The men are still there when he returns. One of the men hands him several folded dollar bills. Marlon gives the man the bag.

Another transaction completed.

Though Marlon has what he calls a successful "business," he has scaled down his drug activity, preferring to do most of the transactions from his apartment. He has shied away from circulating on the streets and doing business at house parties. In Marlon's mind, the money is good enough for him to survive on, but he's still hopeful of getting a job.

Staying home keeps Marlon closer to his music – his number one passion. He spends a lot of his spare time at home rapping with his favorite songs and writing his own lyrics. He and three friends formed a rap group and have visions of producing an album. The group has been going to a studio in downtown Minneapolis four or five times a month for recording sessions.

A couple of hours after Carolyn dropped Marlon off at home, one of the group members, Billy, is walking briskly down the street toward Marlon's building. Billy rushes up the stairs to the second floor and taps excitedly on Marlon's doorbell, hoping his friend is home.

"Who is it?" Marlon yells

"Open up, man! I got some news!" Billy enters the apartment and tells Marlon that their group has been invited to make an appearance on a local cable television show called "Lemme-O-Live," a show that features young artists in the Minneapolis-St. Paul area.

"For real?" Marlon asks.

"Yep," Billy confirms.

After the job disappointment and the lecture from his mother, Marlon can use some good news. Billy's information brings a huge smile to Marlon's face.

Billy and Marlon shake hands and give each other a hug. Billy says the appearance is scheduled for March 4.

The group has about two months to rehearse and get ready for what could be a breakthrough moment.

Marlon begins to see the need to make changes in his life. A potentially big music opportunity is on the horizon and he's about to become a 16 year-old father. His pregnant girlfriend, Carla, is due to have their baby in mid-March. Marlon is giving more thought to going back to school. He enrolled in two alternative high schools after leaving North but quit both. His rationale to his mother for dropping out of the alternative schools: "School is boring." School life was an early indication of Marlon's temperament. He has a history of conflicts in school, including one as a sixth grader in Illinois where he was suspended for throwing a chair at a teacher in a classroom. Marlon was upset that the teacher took the side of the student he was fighting. He was also suspended for fighting as an eighth grader when he attended Northeast Middle School in Minneapolis.

Carolyn was becoming more concerned with Marlon's behavior and suspected he had anger-management problems. She had him see a psychologist when he was 13 to determine if he was bi-polar or dealing with depression.

In some of the school conflicts, Marlon told administrators and his mother that he was coming to the aid of friends who he felt were being bullied. Marlon's compassion for his new Minneapolis friends extended past school hours. He often brought friends home with him who didn't have enough to eat at their house. He would share his mother's cooking and his video games. This was the part of school Marlon enjoyed the most, looking out for friends who didn't have as much as he did.

The TV opportunity and approaching fatherhood is generating a shift in Marlon's thinking about his future. He makes a reversal on his "boring" comment about school. The day after Billy tells him of the TV appearance, Marlon borrows his mother's car, so he and Billy can go to

Plymouth Youth Center to enroll in the current semester.

PYC is one of the alternative schools that Marlon walked out on a few months ago. The PYC receptionist tells Marlon and Billy that enrollment is full but an attempt will be made to get them in. They are told they would have to wait for an opening. Marlon and Billy decide to stay in the lobby and fill out the application. They leave their applications with the receptionist.

Days pass by, then a few weeks. The opening at PYC never materializes for Marlon and Billy. For Marlon, the missed opportunity to get back into PYC is an ominous setback. As for the TV appearance, Marlon misses that dream opportunity as well.

Carolyn was living in Kankakee, Illinois when she decided to move to Minneapolis in October of 1988. Several of Carolyn's close friends had moved to Minneapolis and were trying to get her to join them. When Marlon was younger, Carolyn would bring him along on visits to Minneapolis.

She resisted the move mainly because of Marlon, who enjoyed spending time on Chicago's South Side with some of her family members.

Carolyn would often let Marlon stay with her family on weekends and for several days in the summer.

Marlon was 12 when Carolyn asked him if he wanted to move to Minneapolis. To Carolyn's surprise, he said yes. If Marlon had said he wanted to stay in Illinois, Carolyn was not going to move. She left the decision up to him.

Carolyn's friends had been telling her that Minneapolis would be a better place to raise her son.

The schools are better, the cost of living is affordable and there are more career opportunities. In 1988, the Minneapolis area was home to numerous major corporations, including Northwest Airlines, Target, Best Buy, General Mills, Honeywell, Medtronic, 3M, Blue Cross Blue Shield and many others.

The music scene wasn't bad either. Hometown product Prince had become an international superstar and other local entertainers were enjoying phenomenal success as well, such as The Time, SOS Band, Alexander O'Neal and Sheila E. Time band members Jimmy Jam Harris and Terry Lewis were beginning to branch out with their own production company, Flyte Tyme Productions. The duo was bringing some of the biggest names in the music industry to Minneapolis to produce their songs – Janet Jackson, New Edition, Patti LaBelle,

Luther Van Dross, Larry Graham (formerly of Sly and The Family Stone), Boyz II Men, George Michael, Mariah Carey, Chaka Khan, Tevin Campbell and others. From a business and entertainment perspective, things were booming in Minneapolis. It was an ideal time for Carolyn to consider moving to the city. Shortly after moving to Minneapolis, Carolyn gets a job at a company that prints labels on baby bottles. In less than a year, she was promoted to quality control manager.

When she started with the company, the labels would often remind her of Marlon's early days as an infant in Illinois. Carolyn had a difficult pregnancy before giving birth to Marlon on Oct. 13, 1976 at Ingalls Memorial Hospital in Harvey, Illinois. High blood pressure and heart issues forced Carolyn to spend the final three months of her pregnancy in the hospital. She had to be fed through a tube. There was concern from the doctors that Carolyn and her baby might not survive. Because of the difficult pregnancy, and Marlon surviving, Carolyn was determined to provide for Marlon as much as she could, giving him everything he wanted or needed. In other words, Carolyn was willing to spoil her son and be a strong, attentive mother.

Most mothers would do the same thing after going through a similar experience. Who could blame Carolyn for having that level of passion for motherhood? She came close to missing out on the joys and blessings of raising a child.

A year after Marlon was born, Carolyn was hired as a truck driver, which occasionally took her on the road to make deliveries. On every trip, she packed up Marlon and carried him with her. She did not want to be separated from him. It was one of her early missions as a parent to take Marlon with her whenever possible, a motherly instinct she maintained as Marlon grew older but would ultimately change her life forever.

Laramiun as an adult at 20.

To love means loving the unlovable. To forgive means pardoning the unpardonable. Faith means believing the unbelievable. Hope means hoping when everything seems hopeless.

G.K. Chesterton

# CHAPTER THREE

*A Fateful Intersection – The House Party*

*Thursday, Feb. 11, 1993*

Carolyn is trying to get through a busy Thursday, running errands and making preparations to travel the next morning to Crystal Springs, Miss., where her father died last week. Her father remained in Crystal Springs after she was born there in 1957.

Family members in Mississippi asked her to make the trip to help settle legal matters with her father's estate and his property. Three days earlier, she purchased a roundtrip train ticket with Amtrak and reserved a rental car in Jackson, Miss., to drive to Crystal Springs.

Carolyn's train is scheduled to leave Minneapolis at 5:30 a.m. Friday morning, so she's already planning to turn in early Thursday night after wrapping up a hectic day. She doesn't want to oversleep. Before heading home, she has a dinner outing Thursday evening with two of her friends. The ladies want to spend time with her before she goes to Mississippi.

On the way home after dinner, Carolyn gets a call from her best friend, Angela, who wants to stop by Carolyn's apartment to see her before she leaves town. Carolyn tells Angela she'll be home around 9.

Angela arrives at Carolyn's apartment before Carolyn, but Marlon is home and lets her in. A few of Marlon's friends are at the apartment playing video games with him in his bedroom – Billy, Billy's older brother, Willis; Ralph and Adrienne, a female acquaintance of Marlon. Carolyn enters the apartment carrying several plastic bags from various shopping stops.

Angela gives Carolyn a hug. Fatigued, Carolyn flops down on her couch to rest her legs and relax while talking with Angela.

About 15 minutes later, Carolyn gets a call from Teresa, a friend of a man who Carolyn used to date. Teresa calls to tell Carolyn about an "after hours" party she was going to in North Minneapolis. Carolyn tells Teresa she's leaving town early in the morning and doesn't want to go anywhere. Carolyn writes down the address of the house but is still firm in her plans to stay home.

Angela overhears the conversation. After Carolyn hangs up from talking to Teresa, Angela tries to convince Carolyn to go to the party. "Girl, let's just go for a few," Angela tells Carolyn. "You're leaving tomorrow. I won't see you for a while."

"Girl, I'm tired," Carolyn responds. "You go."

Angela and Carolyn go back and forth about the party for several minutes before Carolyn gives in and says yes. Carolyn insists on getting more of her packing done and cleaning up her kitchen before heading out to the party. Angela agrees to help.

It's a few minutes past midnight. Carolyn has most of her packing done. Even while packing and tidying up her kitchen, Carolyn is wrestling with second thoughts about going to the party. But she doesn't want to break her promise to Angela. She and Angela grab their jackets and purses.

Carolyn walks to Marlon's bedroom, where the video games are still going strong with his friends. She tells Marlon and his friends where she and Angela are going. All eyes remain focused on the TV screen until Carolyn looks directly at Marlon and says, "You want to go?"

Carolyn's maternal instincts to take her son along, just as she did when Marlon was younger, surface again. Only this time, Marlon is 16 and the destination is an after-hours party for adults.

Billy is the first to answer Carolyn's question. "I want to go!"

Marlon pauses his video controller and looks at his mother. "Yeah, I'll go!"

Marlon then turns to his friends. "Ya'll want to go?"

Willis and Adrienne say yes.

Ralph passes on the invitation and says he's going home.

Marlon shuts down the video game as everyone hurriedly gets themselves together to head out.

Carolyn and Angela suddenly have four passengers going with them to the party in Carolyn's white, four-door 98 Oldsmobile.

Carolyn has one more thing to say to Marlon as she walks toward the front door with Angela, "Make sure you leave that damn gun at home!"

Marlon and Billy are the only people left in Marlon's bedroom when they hear Carolyn's order. They look at each other and don't say anything. The eye contact is all the direction Billy needs on what to do. Billy reaches into Marlon's stereo system and pulls out a .25-caliber semi-automatic pistol. Billy puts the gun in his jacket pocket.

Marlon routinely carries a gun wherever he goes because of his gang and drug activities.

He never likes to leave home without it. He feels safer. In his mind, however, he's following his mother's orders – the gun is in Billy's pocket. Not his.

Carolyn is driving the group to the party, unaware that Marlon and Billy have not followed her instructions. During the 15-minute drive to the house, Carolyn has no second thoughts about bringing Marlon and his young friends. Teresa mentioned to her on the phone that there might be a few young people at the party for Marlon and his friends to socialize with.

Carolyn finds a parking space near the house. As the group approaches the front steps, they hear the music. There definitely is a party happening inside.

When the group enters the house through the front door, they see about 15 people. All are in the living room or nearby dining room.

Moments after walking into the house, Marlon makes eye contact with a man he has never seen before. Billy notices the brief stare-down as he and Marlon make their way toward the dining room.

"You know that dude?" Billy asks.

Marlon replies, "Nah, don't know him."

Marlon and Billy help themselves to some snacks on the table and ask for a drink, but the eye contact didn't sit well with Marlon, who says to himself softly, "What the f-- is he looking at?"

While Marlon and Billy are in the dining room area, Carolyn, Angela, Willis and Adrienne are mingling in the living room.

After a song fades out, a popular hip-hop tune comes on that has everyone in the house bobbing their heads to the beat.

Marlon and Billy, still in the dining room area, are bobbing their heads and begin to make casual dance moves. As part of their moves, Marlon and Billy make hand gestures that symbolize their affiliation with the Gangster Disciples street gang. On the streets, the hand gestures are known as "stacking."

The man who had made eye contact with Marlon when he entered the house sees Marlon and Billy stacking their gang signs to each other. The man approaches them, making "stacking" signs associated with the infamous Crips street gang. Within seconds, the dining room becomes a miniature battleground for members of two rival street gangs.

The man moves toward Billy, igniting a heated argument between the two. Marlon steps forward to defend his friend and begins to argue with the man. All three are face to face loudly cursing the other's gang affiliation.

"F— a Gangster!"

"F— a Crip!"

The shouting can be heard above the music.

Other people at the party, including Carolyn and Angela, move in to break up the friction before it gets physical. Marlon is ready to fight the man and poised to throw a punch. That instinct to help a friend still exists within Marlon. The fact that it's a gang issue makes Marlon react even quicker – and with more hostility.

As the atmosphere settles down and everyone resumes what they were doing, Angela calmly says to the man Marlon was about to fight, "That's my friend's son…I don't think you want to mess with him…"

The man gives no response. He turns away and heads toward the kitchen to get a drink.

Carolyn and Angela go into the living room to sit on a couch with their drinks.

Marlon and Billy remain standing with their drinks and snacks but move closer to the living room, standing along the wall to avoid blocking anyone's path toward the dining room.

Everything appears to be cool. The hip-hop music continues to play. A few people are dancing. Others are drinking, eating and talking. But several minutes later, tensions escalate again.

The man who was arguing with Marlon and Billy goes into the living room and taps Carolyn's leg, then Angela's leg. He sits down between them on the couch, forcing the two ladies to move over slightly.

Marlon doesn't see the man tap his mother's leg or Angela's, but moments later, he notices the man sitting between them.

The man attempts to start a conversation with Carolyn and Angela, "Hey ladies! How ya'll doing?" the man says.

Carolyn and Angela look at each other smiling.

"Well, it's time to go," Carolyn says to Angela.

Without answering the man's question, Carolyn and Angela stand up and prepare to go outside to get some fresh air. Carolyn remembers the previous altercation the man had with her son, plus she can tell the man is much younger than her. Carolyn is 36. She's hoping to avoid further drama by not engaging in any discussion with the man.

The man quickly stands up and positions himself between Carolyn and Angela. "Oh, ya'll don't want to know my name?" he asks. He looks over at Carolyn. "What's your name?"

Before Carolyn can respond, Angela answers, "My name is Angela."

The man looks at Angela but points his finger to Carolyn. "Not you, I'm talking to her."

"My name is Carolyn."

The man introduces himself, smiling and rotating his head slightly to emphasize his name. "My name is La-ra-mi-un…Can you say my name?"

Carolyn quickly says his name with the intent of ending the conversation and heading to the door, but the man persists.

"Wow, you're very punctual and very articulate!"

Carolyn and Angela laugh and then walk to the door to go outside. Carolyn hears Laramiun saying one more line as they walk away from him, "Oh, ya'll don't want to get to know me?"

Carolyn and Angela keep walking. Neither lady turns around to respond. Carolyn is hoping her group is ready to go home as she and Angela get outside. She, Angela, and Laramiun, are unaware that Marlon, still fuming from his previous confrontation with the man he doesn't know, has been observing the brief conversation between the three from across the room.

After Carolyn and Angela go outside, Laramiun is standing by himself in front of the couch sipping on his drink. He and Marlon make eye contact again.

Billy is standing next to Marlon but doesn't notice that Marlon and Laramiun are having another stare-down. Laramiun walks toward Marlon, shouting, "What's up?"

Marlon says the same thing to Laramiun, "What's up?"

Billy hears Marlon's response and moves behind Marlon as he and Laramiun are in each other's face again. This time, they're in the living room and people aren't close enough to get in between them. The argument gets more intense. Billy is standing directly behind Marlon. Billy's right hand is in his pocket. His hand has a grip on the gun that wasn't supposed to be with him or Marlon.

Laramiun takes a couple of steps back and yells at Marlon, "What you gonna do?"

Billy nudges Marlon. Marlon extends his right hand backwards and feels Billy place the gun in his hand.

As Marlon wraps his hand around the gun, he thinks he sees Laramiun make a suspicious move, as if he's reaching for something. Marlon brings his arm forward with the gun in his hand. He raises the gun and fires four shots into Laramiun's body.

Laramiun's chest and neck take direct hits and he crumples to the floor.

Other people hit the floor as well. Women at the party are screaming. People scramble to get out of the house.

Carolyn and Angela, still outside, hear the commotion and rush to the steps of the house to see what's going on. Carolyn hears what she thought were firecrackers.

She is mistaken.

Marlon, Billy, Adrienne and Willis are rushing out of the house as Carolyn and Angela get to the steps. "Momma, I'm all right," Marlon says to his mother.

As screams continue inside the house, the group rushes to get inside Carolyn's car.

Carolyn turns the ignition and speeds off. No one is talking.

Marlon is sitting in the front seat with his mother. A red traffic light gives Carolyn a moment to look at her son. He appears agitated as he stares out the passenger window.

Carolyn doesn't say anything to Marlon. She just looks at him. Her eyes begin to water. Tears trickle down her face. The look on her son's face scares her but she's afraid to ask what happened. Her maternal instincts are telling her that something terrible went down in the house, and her son was inside at the time.

The red light seems much longer than usual, long enough for a number of concerning thoughts to race through Carolyn's mind as she looks over at Marlon. Did my son see what happened? Was he involved? Why does he look so angry? WHAT

THE HELL HAPPENED IN THERE? If Carolyn wanted to ask these questions, she couldn't. The fear of the moment is keeping the words from coming out of her mouth.

The car remains silent, except for the distant sound of sirens in the background. No one is talking. When the light changes to green, Carolyn turns away from her son, without saying a word, and resumes the drive home.

Mary's sentimental lockett.

*Forgiveness* is not always easy. At times, it feels more painful than the wound we suffered, to forgive the one that inflicted it. And yet, there is no peace without forgiveness.

# CHAPTER FOUR

## *Mary's routine day erupts into heartache*

*Friday, February 12, 1993*

Early Friday morning, at 3:58 a.m., Laramiun Lamont Byrd, Mary's only child, is pronounced dead at North Memorial Hospital. He was 20.

Three men, including the man who hosted the after-hours party at his house, rushed Laramiun to North Memorial in one of the men's car. Laramiun is unconscious in the backseat and bleeding.

The drive to the suburban Minneapolis hospital is five minutes from the house, but the short distance will not make a difference. The four bullets have done too much damage for the emergency room trauma team to save him.

Another life expires because of an argument over gang affiliation. The argument had nothing to do with a turf war, selling drugs on the wrong block. Or being on the wrong block by accident. Or wearing a color not welcome in a certain neighborhood. Laramiun and Marlon were not wearing their gang colors.

The house party just happened to be the intersection where their gang signals crossed paths. Simple eye contact started it all. Both individuals accepted the challenge of flexing strong in the name of Gangster Disciples or Crips, and neither wanted to show the appearance of weakness. In most cases, these showdowns leave no room for rational thinking or peace-making. Laramiun and Marlon's fatal confrontation could have happened anywhere—at a place where the innocent can end up dead in the crossfire. It happens.

To many people, the hand gestures displayed by Laramiun and Marlon seem such a trivial reason to spark a homicide. In the African-American community, it's a somber reminder, an almost daily example of how life seems to have such limited value.

An hour and a half after doctors pronounced Laramiun dead, Carolyn boards an Amtrak train for Jackson, Miss. She's exhausted physically and mentally – and worried about her son.

She still has no idea of the extent of Marlon's involvement in what happened at the party.

*Three hours have passed since doctors at North Memorial proclaim, "Nothing more can be done" for Laramiun.*

Mary is having a playful moment in front of her bathroom mirror, as she gets ready for work. She poses a few times like a model while putting on her makeup, thanking God in the process for waking her up. Though she's multi-tasking, she continues her cheerful conversation with Her Lord and Savior, "Father, I'm so glad you told me to keep my mouth shut at church last night. That Francine was working my last nerve in our meeting…Talkin' about how this guy wants to take her on a cruise and this *'other'* guy likes to take her shopping. I like going shopping too but I can buy my *own* clothes! Thank you very much! We don't need to hear all that nonsense about her men! You didn't hear this from me, but I think she's doing a lot more than worshipping You!"

Regardless of her mood, Mary starts each day talking and praying to God as she gets dressed for work. She is particularly upbeat this morning because it's Friday. The weekend awaits and she'll be in her US West office all day. No community events are scheduled today and none tomorrow. She has a free weekend coming up. A quick glance at her bathroom clock tells Mary it's time to go and wish God a good day. "You have a wonderful day My Lord!"

Mary's co-worker, Diane, is pulling up outside of Mary's house to give her a ride. Diane stops by every morning to pick her up. Mary's North Minneapolis home is near Diane's travel route. They work together on US West's North Side Community Service team. Diane is in a good mood as well this morning when Mary gets into the car. "Girl, I went to see 'Groundhog Day' last night with Bill Murray...It was so funny!"

"Girl, I was in church last night," Mary said.

"Church?"

"Yeah, we had one of our women's group meetings. You should come sometime."

"Mary, I get all the gossip I need from the women at work!"

"We don't be gossiping!"

Mary pauses. "...Not all the time!"

Mary and Diane laugh together. They continue to have a lively chat on their way to work.

Mary has no idea that her life has taken a heartbreaking, wrong-way turn.

Mary settles into her cubicle at 8 a.m. and begins going over paperwork for 1-800 orders and future community events. Like clockwork, her phone rings at 8:20 a.m. Every morning at this time, Mary gets a call from Annette, a close friend and co-worker who works across the street in US West's second building. Annette, a mobile repair person, has known Mary for seven years. She joined Mary's church after an invite from Mary one Sunday. She's been going to church with Mary ever since.

Whenever Annette calls in the morning, she and Mary chit-chat, share the latest gossip, laugh a little, then open up their Bibles and read a verse together. Mary and Annette take turns each day on selecting what verse they will read. After their brief Bible moment, it's back to work.

Annette calls Mary back around 11:30 to tell her she's going to lunch and asks Mary if she wants her to bring her something. Mary declines, telling Annette she'll get something later.

Fifteen minutes after passing on Annette's lunch invitation, Mary gets a call from her sister-in-law, Edwina.

Edwina got a call from her sister who works at The City Inc. an alternative school in Minneapolis. Edwina's sister called her after hearing something about Laramiun. "Hey Mary, do you know if Laramiun came home last night?" Edwina asked.

"I don't know."

"If you needed to get in touch with him, can you?"

Mary is confused about Edwina's question. "Why are you asking me that way?"

"My sister at City Inc. told me Laramiun is dead."

"What! Let me talk to your sister." Mary is calm but feels concerned.

Edwina's sister comes on the phone. She speaks to Mary briefly and transfers the call to a female co-worker who has more information. "Hello, this is Mrs. Watson. Miss Johnson, I got a call from somebody who told me that Laramiun was killed. I'm sorry. I don't know any more than that."

"How do you know this about my child? I don't understand what you're talking about. I need to call somebody to check on this." Mary hangs up the phone and calls her sister Mildred. Laramiun has been living at Mildred's house in North Minneapolis. Mary is hopeful her sister can clear this up.

"Edwina and a lady at The City Inc. are telling me Laramiun is dead."

"Oh, my God!" Mildred gasps

"I still don't know if it's true or not," Mary tells her.

"Don't worry, Mary! I'll call North Memorial to find out if they know anything. I'll call you back."

Diane's desk is right behind Mary's cubicle. She's been hearing the concern in Mary's voice the last couple of minutes and comes over to Mary's cubicle. "Is everything okay?"

Diane sees a troubled look on Mary's face.

"I don't know." Mary's voice trembles. While waiting for Mildred to call her back, Mary calls her nephew, Kevin, who lives down the street from Laramiun's girlfriend. She asks Kevin to go to the girlfriend's house to see if he's there.

"Call me right back," Mary insists.

Kevin calls back 15 minutes later to inform Mary that Laramiun is not at his girlfriend's house. She told Kevin she hasn't seen Laramiun since yesterday.

"What's going on Auntie?" he asks.

Mary's voice trembles again as she tells him, "I'm just trying to find him. Thanks for doing that. I'll let you know what I find out."

Diane continues to stand by Mary's desk as Mary remains seated talking on the phone. She doesn't like the expression on Mary's face. "Is everything okay? What's wrong?"

Mary looks at Diane. Her eyes are beginning to fill with tears. "I'm trying to find Laramiun. Nobody knows where he is."

Mary and Diane talk for a moment.

Mary's phone rings again. She quickly picks it up. It's Mildred. "I called the hospital. They transferred me to the police department. They asked me if I knew what Laramiun was wearing."

Mary's voice gets a little louder: "Why did they want to know that?"

Two other co-workers, including a male supervisor, come over to Mary's cubicle during the conversation. They notice Diane has a worried look on her face while standing at Mary's desk. They sense something is wrong.

Mildred's voice begins to shake as she continues speaking, "I don't know Mary. I told them what he was wearing when he left here. When I told them what he had on, they said they were coming to the house. If it wasn't true, why would they be coming to the house Mary?"

Mary stands up and shouts, "DON'T TELL ME THAT!" The phone suddenly flies out of Mary's hand. A high-pitched scream erupts from her lungs. Mary's body slumps.

Diane and one of the co-workers catch Mary before she falls to the floor, clutching her as she yells Laramiun's name.

Tears roll down Diane's face. Diane and the co-workers ease Mary into her chair.

The entire office comes to a stop. Other co-workers in the area rush over to Mary's cubicle.

One co-worker dashes to get a towel and water. Mary's body is limp as she tries to sit upright in the chair at her desk. Co-workers do their best to comfort her. One of them gives her a cup of water. Another one places a cold towel on her forehead.

Mary has briefly gone into shock, prompting co-workers to consider calling paramedics.

Tears continue to roll down Mary's face.

Diane reaches for the dangling phone and discovers that Mildred is still on the line. Mildred is sobbing too. She heard her sister screaming on the other end.

"Mildred, we have her. We're taking care of her."

"Thank you. Please bring her here when you can."

"No problem. We'll get her there."

Mary doesn't move from her chair for several minutes.

Co-workers continue to give her comfort. One of the co-workers in the department knows Annette and Mary are close friends and places a call across the street. Annette is not back yet from lunch, but the co-worker gives emphatic instructions to have Annette call Mary's phone as soon as she returns.

Moments later in her building, Annette gets off the elevator and is surrounded by her co-workers. As soon as she gets to her desk, one of the men, in a frantic voice, tells Annette: "Call Mary right now!"

"Why?"

"We don't know," the man responds. "Call her! Something's happened over there."

Annette drops her lunch bag on her desk and dials Mary's number.

Diane answers and hears Annette's voice, "Mary, it's Annette!"

Diane gives the phone to Mary. "Mary, it's me, Annette! What's going on?"

"He's dead, Annette…He's dead!"

"Who? Your father?"

"Laramiun."

"What?"

Mary can't talk. Hearing her close friend's voice triggers another blast of emotion. The next thing Annette hears over the phone is Mary's loud scream. When she screams again, Annette begins to cry.

Diane and Lisa, a co-worker, eventually calm Mary enough to drive her to Mildred's house. Laramiun was living with Mildred until he got his own place.

Mildred is standing in the doorway when Diane's car pulls up.

Diane grabs one of Mary's arms and Lisa grabs the other as they walk with her to Mildred's door.

Mary and Mildred have a tearful embrace in the doorway.

"The detectives are here, but they won't tell me if it's Laramiun," Mildred tells Mary.

Mary is silent as Diane and Lisa lead her into the living room toward a couch so she can sit down.

Two detectives dressed in suits politely greet her. One of the detectives informs Mary they have to follow procedures. They can't confirm if it's Laramiun until they hear from the morgue.

"I understand," Mary says softly.

While Mary is talking with the detectives, two of Laramiun's friends come to Mildred's house. One of the detectives asks the young men about the last time they saw Laramiun. They tell the detective that they were with Laramiun at a party last night about three blocks from here.

Mary and Mildred look at each other and shake their heads in disbelief.

The detectives tell Mary and Mildred that they need to go to the location of the party to check it out. They said they would come back to Mildred's house within an hour.

Diane and Lisa stay with Mary after the detectives leave. The detectives return about a half-hour later to gather more information.

A few minutes later, one of the detectives gets a call. He steps outside for a moment, then comes back into the living room. "Miss Johnson…That was the morgue. I'm sorry to have to tell you this. We do have a confirmation. They identified the body as your son. We're sorry for your loss."

Mildred cries out, "Oh, my God! No!"

Mary is seated on the couch between Diane and Lisa. Both grab her hands. Diane and Lisa start crying and hugging Mary.

Mary's face is expressionless. She tries to process what she just heard about her son. She gets up from the couch and walks slowly to the bathroom, closing the door behind her. Mary's bathroom at home is where she and God have their conversations every morning. Although Mary is in Mildred's bathroom, it is still the sanctuary she needs to get answers from Her Savior.

"Lord, what is going on?" Mary asks. "I do what you tell me to do! I know Laramiun wasn't living his life the way I raised him. Why Lord? Why?"

Mary pauses as if she's waiting for an answer. She then hears a voice that only she can hear...

*"I've done what you asked me to do...I have him."*

Mary leading community members in an anti-violence march in North Minneapolis.

# CHAPTER FIVE

### *Marlon's arrest; Mary buries her son*

Twelve hours have passed since Marlon shot and killed a man he didn't know. Marlon is laying low at the home of his mother's ex-boyfriend in North Minneapolis. He and his mother's ex still have a good relationship, which is paying off in a valuable way today. The ex doesn't mind Marlon staying with him for a few days.

Marlon's street instincts tell him it's not a good idea to stay at his mother's apartment.

Too many people know where he lives.

Marlon stays in the house all day. Later in the afternoon, he begins to get page messages on his phone from friends who tell him they heard what happened last night. They said Billy told them. The fact that Billy is spreading the news irritates Marlon, but there's nothing he can do about it. He doesn't want to go outside looking for Billy to tell him to keep his mouth shut.

Out of curiosity, Marlon changes the TV channel at 5 o'clock to watch the local news to see if there's any coverage of the shooting last night. It doesn't take long to find out. The station he's watching reports on two stories before telling viewers about a fatal shooting that happened last night at a house party in North Minneapolis..."

Marlon is not identified as the gunman, but he knows the story is about him. The word is out that Minneapolis police are looking for a suspect and have asked witnesses or people with information to come forward or call the police tip line.

Two days pass and Marlon has not left his mother's ex-boyfriend's home. Marlon is getting more frustrated that he can't get around. He often drives his mother's car, but he feels it would be too risky to go home and use it to go places. His mother's car was at the house party and might have been identified as the group sped off after the shooting.

At 16, Marlon's chances of living a productive life – at least finishing high school or perhaps going to college – are severely diminished. He's the latest suspected criminal targeted by the Minneapolis Police. Even if he avoids capture for an extended period, he will have to be careful where he goes and who he associates with. He's beginning to worry more about Billy talking too much.

There were people at the party who saw Marlon and Laramiun arguing before the shooting. They could be talking as well, maybe not to the police, but to family and friends. The time could come when all the conversation about what happened at that house party would eventually lead authorities to Marlon. No matter the level of Marlon's street sense, avoiding apprehension won't be easy because of witnesses.

How long can Marlon lay low? Does he have enough resources to stay a step ahead of the police? At his age, the odds are against Marlon to come up with a positive answer to both questions.

*February 15, 1993*

It's Monday afternoon. Marlon is fed up with life underground. He spent the entire weekend in the house, occasionally replaying in his mind what happened at the party. Marlon shows no signs of remorse or regret. A rival gang member got in his face twice and also interacted with his mother. For Marlon, those circumstances add up to standing his ground and letting people know he's not soft.

A timely phone call comes in from Alvin Blair, a friend of Marlon's mother. The call gives Marlon the excuse he needs to get out of the house. Alvin asks Marlon if he can use his mother's car to take lunch to his girlfriend at her job.

Marlon consents, plus he's hungry. Before putting on his heavy jacket, he reaches inside a jacket pocket to feel for his gun. It's in there – the same gun he and Billy had with them at the party. The gun is loaded.

Marlon is about to step outside for the first time since the party. After what happened three nights ago, he feels even more uncomfortable about leaving the house without his piece.

Just in case there is a "revenge warrant" on the streets, Marlon wants to have protection. He's not sure how much Billy has said to people about the shooting and who he has talked to. Marlon knows how fast "news" can travel in the streets. If the wrong person hears about the shooting, and that person happens to be a friend of the guy he shot, or worse yet, a fellow gang member, the conversation trail could lead to Marlon quicker than expected.

As Marlon walks out the door, the chilling words of his mother from Thursday night ring in his ears again, *"Make sure you leave that damn gun at home!"*

Marlon hesitates but he keeps going. Ignoring his mother's demand once more leads to another fateful moment. He walks several blocks to his mother's apartment to meet up with Alvin. Marlon goes inside to get the keys to her car, which is parked in the rear of the building.

He lets Alvin drive. Marlon tells Alvin he can keep the car until his mother comes back from Mississippi. Allowing Alvin to keep the car is part of Marlon's strategy to minimize suspicion at his mother's apartment in case the police are looking for the vehicle.

The first stop is Kentucky Fried Chicken on Broadway, a street that goes through a business district in North Minneapolis, then to Alvin's girlfriend's job at a nearby office building.

Marlon eats his lunch order in the car, while Alvin goes inside to deliver a KFC meal to his girlfriend.

Alvin is inside his girlfriend's office building for more than 30 minutes, making Marlon feel a little edgy. He's wondering why Alvin is taking so long. Alvin finally returns and asks Marlon where he wants to go. Marlon says he wants to stop at a nearby liquor store before going back to his mother's ex-boyfriend's house.

After the liquor store run, Alvin drives Marlon to the ex-boyfriend's house. Marlon is wondering why Alvin isn't as talkative as he was earlier. Alvin was chatty with Marlon when they got into the car, asking Marlon about how his mother was doing in Mississippi and how Marlon's rap group is doing. Alvin is familiar with Marlon's music interests.

The lack of conversation all of a sudden raises a mild concern with Marlon, but he doesn't get a chance to figure it out or ask Alvin if something's on his mind.

Marlon notices two cars make a U-turn behind them. Both cars continue to follow them as they head toward the ex-boyfriend's house. Alvin pulls up in front of the house and Marlon gets out. As soon as Marlon closes the passenger door and is clear of the car, Alvin drives off without saying anything.

The two cars behind them quickly pull up and stop in the middle of the street. Several men from both cars rush out with guns drawn, yelling "Police! Freeze! Hands up!"

The men are plain clothes policemen traveling in unmarked Minneapolis police vehicles. All of the officers have their arms extended in a rigid straight line, pointing their guns directly at Marlon.

He knows he can't afford to make a wrong move. Marlon freezes. His hands go up, shaking his head in disgust. He's ordered to turn around.

Handcuffs immobilize his arms. An officer reads Marlon his rights and says he's being arrested on suspicion of first-degree murder. While the officer is reading Marlon his rights, another one is patting him down. The officer feels a familiar object as he touches one of Marlon's jacket pockets. The officer pulls out the gun.

Marlon's concerns are justified. It all adds up – Alvin's lengthy stay at his girlfriend's job, Alvin's silence after leaving the liquor store and the two cars making the quick U-turn. The set-up flowed like clockwork. Marlon theorizes that Alvin spent extra time at his girlfriend's job alerting police that Marlon was with him. Marlon later finds out that Alvin knew the man he fatally shot at the house party. Alvin had heard about the shooting and was told that Marlon pulled the trigger.

The police take Marlon into custody at Hennepin County Jail. Bail is set at $250,000. No one in Marlon's family or anybody he knows is able to post bail for him, so Marlon, living in Minneapolis for only five years, is facing an extensive jail term and a future that doesn't have much promise. He remains in jail until the start of his trial next year.

Later in the evening, one of the detectives who came to Mildred's house on Friday calls Mary to tell her police arrested a 16 year old boy in connection with Laramiun's death.

The news does little to raise Mary's spirits. Mary stayed at Mildred's house over the weekend, unable to build the strength to go home. She ends up staying the entire week at Mildred's.

Mary has had no appetite while she's been at Mildred's. She has gone the whole week without eating. She forced herself to drink coffee each day. Diane brought Mary a pistachio dish, one of Mary's favorite meals, but she doesn't eat it until after the funeral. Mary simply isn't hungry. Her grief has replaced whatever hunger pains that normally would be tugging at her body.

Family and friends have been in and out of Mildred's house to comfort Mary since news of Laramiun's death spread on Friday. Neighbors near Mary's house leave notes of condolences on her porch. Laramiun's death is another reminder of how violent crimes continue to shatter the North Minneapolis community. Some fatal crimes in the area go unsolved for lack of evidence or fear among witnesses to come forward to help the police. Laramiun's death is not falling into either category. It appears the police had some assistance in tracking down Marlon.

Mary is the latest mother in the community to lose a child to violence. She often worried about Laramiun's safety because of his drug activity, but she never imagined that a house party would lead to her worst fears. At the moment, Mary has no idea about what happened at the party and why. All she knows is that Laramiun is gone, and she won't get to see him on that fishing boat he dreamed of buying. His dreams have been replaced by funeral arrangements.

*Friday, Feburary 19, 1993*

Family members have assisted Mary throughout the past week in planning Laramiun's services. The visitation was last night. The memorial service and burial is scheduled for today, exactly one week after his death.

Mary is in Mildred's bathroom getting ready for the memorial service. Her face is pale. Her eyes are weak from tears and pain. Her movements around Mildred's house are slow. Mary's mood is visibly shaped by grief, but she maintains her morning ritual of talking to God in the bathroom.

On this morning, however, there's more prayer than a conversation. Mary is asking for strength and guidance to get through this day, the last day she will see her son.

Mildred's house is busy with family members moving around preparing to go with Mary to the memorial. Mary doesn't hear the activity and conversations. She has tuned it all out as she attempts to get as close as she can to her Lord and Savior. If there ever was a moment where Mary needed spiritual support, today is the day.

Mildred approaches the bathroom entrance to check on Mary. She sees Mary standing in front of the mirror praying. Mildred doesn't interrupt her sister. She stands in the doorway looking at Mary. Mildred clasps her hands together and closes her eyes, speaking softly as if she's praying with her sister.

Mary concludes her prayer and sees Mildred in the mirror standing in the doorway.

As she turns around, Mildred walks toward Mary to give her a tender embrace. "Come on Mary. It's time to go...We're all with you."

The limousines from Estes Funeral Home have pulled up to take the family to the service. When the group arrives at the funeral home, they wait momentarily in the lobby before proceeding into the chapel.

From the lobby, Mary can see Laramiun's body in the casket. The sight of Laramiun stirs emotions in Mary. Her eyes tear up as she stares at the casket. The lobby of this funeral home is the last place she expected to be on this chilly, overcast morning. It's 19 degrees outside, but nothing is colder than the agony of burying your only child.

Though numerous people are standing in the lobby with Mary, she zones out and shuts down the nearby idle chatter among family and friends. Silence surrounds her. All she hears and sees are conversations she used to have with Laramiun at the dinner table, the living room, and even in his bedroom when he was a young boy, when Mary is about to tuck him in after they say a prayer together. Mary can see Laramiun smiling back at her as he lay under the covers in his bed.

Mary's flashbacks of Laramiun continue to play on her internal video screen until Mildred pauses the moment with a gentle tap on her arm. The tap brings Mary back to the lobby and lets her know it's time for the procession to make a solemn walk into the chapel.

The chapel is filled with people on both sides of the aisle. Tears stream down Mary's face, as she and the procession get closer to the casket. When she reaches the casket, she gets a full view of Laramiun, slowly shaking her head in disbelief. Her legs weaken.

Family members clutch her arms and lead her to a chair in the front row.

Mary needs to sit down. The up-close view of Laramiun overwhelms her.

Time has been set aside during the service for people to offer remarks and testimonials about Laramiun.

After about 15 minutes of remarks, Mary is helped out of her seat and makes her way to the podium. Making no mention of the crime that took her son's life, Mary focuses her brief comments on the young people attending the service, "All of you need to make the right choices on what you're doing with your life," Mary says. "It can all be taken away in an instant. Don't let your parents go through what I'm going through right now. Spare your parents from this heartache…"

Mary speaks a few more minutes about how the young people in the audience should be living their lives. She didn't expect such a huge turnout of young people who knew her son. Many individuals are forced to listen to the service outside. The chapel is filled to capacity. The strong showing of young people motivates Mary to give more of a lecture than special memories of her son. She believes it's the right thing to do. Mary's hope is that her message will inspire troubled, young persons to re-examine their lives and make a change – not only for themselves but for their families as well.

As much as Mary is dealing with the heartache of losing Laramiun, her brief speech to the young people in the audience represents an awakening inside of Mary, a side rarely seen in her personality. Mary tells anyone she's soft-spoken and occasionally shy, but Laramiun's death appears to have ignited a change in her demeanor – and willingness to talk in public.

At the cemetery later in the afternoon, Mary pays a final tribute to Laramiun by singing

"Going Through The Motions," a 1983 song by the rock band Kansas. Some of the lyrics in the song must have reminded Mary about her concerns with Laramiun's lifestyle while he was growing up and the numerous chats she had with him to change his ways.

*'And is your day just a reflection of the day before?*

*Don't you ever stop and wonder if there's something more?'*

A minister offers final remarks and prayer to conclude the burial service, then Mary and others lay flowers on Laramiun's casket before turning and walking slowly away from the gravesite. More tears trickle down Mary's face as family members, holding her arms, flank her for the walk back to the funeral cars. Mary raises her head slightly. Her eyes are riveted, looking straight ahead as if she's locked in on an object. A significant shift of emotion is evident in Mary's eyes – from sorrow to defiance.

Ray H. Richardson

Mary participating in a prayer vigil with the Visitation
Sisters of Minneapolis.

HOLDING A GRUDGE DOESN'T MAKE YOU STRONG; IT MAKES YOU BITTER. FORGIVING DOESN'T MAKE YOU WEAK; IT SETS YOU FREE.

DAVEWILLIS.ORG

# CHAPTER SIX

## *A quick trial; a guilty verdict*

*Oct. 12, 1994*

It's the eighth day, and most likely, the final day of a murder trial in Hennepin County's Fourth Judicial District Court: The State of Minnesota vs. Marlon Rockshawn Green.

Judge William B. Christensen was informed late yesterday that the jury was expected to reach a verdict today in the second-degree murder case against Marlon for fatally shooting Laramiun Byrd.

Prosecutors were originally pursuing first-degree charges. A conviction would result in a life sentence without chance of parole. Christensen reduced the charge in the summer to second degree murder because Marlon was 16 when the crime was committed. Marlon, now 17, has spent the last 19 months in Hennepin County Jail awaiting trial.

Lowering the charge represented the only positive development in Marlon's defense.

Evidence and testimony heard over the previous seven days are weighing heavily against him.

Witnesses at the party testified they saw Marlon and Laramiun arguing several minutes before the shooting. The initial argument served as probable cause and a potential motive for the shooting, even though Marlon and Laramiun did not know each other.

Prosecutors also have the advantage of Adrienne's key testimony. Adrienne testified she was standing next to Marlon in the living room of the house and saw him shoot Laramiun when they were arguing a second time.

Marlon's attorney, Richard Leroy, is countering with a "heat of passion" defense. Leroy argued that Marlon acted in defense of his mother, who Marlon believed was being "threatened" by Laramiun. Marlon reiterated that claim when he took the stand in his defense. Leroy, however, was unable to provide substantial evidence that Carolyn was in a threatening situation. Carolyn and Angela did have a brief conversation with Laramiun at the party, but Carolyn cut it short, opting to go outside with Angela to avoid any further issues with the man who previously was arguing with her son.

During Adrienne's testimony, she was asked by Hennepin County attorney Judith Harrigan if she heard threatening comments from Laramiun toward Carolyn. Adrienne said no.

The strong case against Marlon appears to be a primary reason the jury is ready to deliver a verdict after only seven days of testimony.

Mary has been in the courtroom for all seven days of the trial, accompanied by two of her aunts, Louise and Anna.

Carolyn has been there each day as well.

The tension between Mary and Carolyn nearly erupts today when both mothers are in a lobby area outside the courtroom waiting for the verdict.

Mary is sitting with her aunts; Carolyn and Leroy are sitting about 30 feet away to the left.

Mary leans forward and looks at Carolyn. She can no longer contain her feelings. "What kind of mother are you?...taking your son to a party like that," Mary says with anger in her voice.

"What kind of mother are you?" Carolyn fires back.

Mary gasps and yells, "Don't talk to me about what kind of mother I am!"

Carolyn: "Who are YOU to be asking me?"

Mary stands up and takes a few steps toward Carolyn before her aunts get in front of her.

Carolyn is also up and moving toward Mary. Leroy intervenes and stops Carolyn.

Mary and Carolyn give each other a cold stare before Leroy convinces Carolyn to turn around and walk with him. He leads her to a waiting area further away from the courtroom – and from Mary.

Carolyn's back is turned, but Mary's eyes remain fixed on Carolyn and Leroy until they turn a corner in the hallway. The trial has made Mary bitter and angry again. Her temper is short. Mary has gradually moved beyond the daily heartaches of losing her son a year and a half ago, but details and accounts of what happened that night at the party have brought back unsettling memories for her. Seeing Carolyn at the trial each day hasn't made things any easier for Mary.

In Mary's mind, Carolyn is the reason her son is dead.

The way Carolyn sees it, Mary's son was the agitator who wouldn't leave Marlon alone.

In the aftermath of a murder, two mothers are dealing with their own personal conflict. One of the sons is still alive, but both mothers will be tragically connected forever. Pain, misery and the unknown will be their links. No matter which way the jury rules, this case will not render peace and comfort for either mother.

Sadly, this scenario has too many daily episodes around the nation. Whenever a life is taken by a criminal act, there will likely be two mothers sharing the pain – the mother of the victim and the mother of the offender. An offender's mother also suffers a loss if her son or daughter is convicted of the homicide and sent away to prison – in some cases for life. For the mother of a homicide victim, a conviction is a hollow victory. She will never see her son or daughter again.

Mary doesn't realize it now, but her stare-down with Carolyn, a symbol of two hurting mothers, is the catalyst for a powerful movement down the road.

Mary and Carolyn have simmered down by the time a court officer comes out of the courtroom to inform Mary and her aunts that the jury is ready to announce its verdict.

"Where is Miss Green?" the officer asks.

"She's down there somewhere," Mary mumbles as she goes inside the courtroom.

The officer walks down the hall to find Carolyn and Leroy.

Mary and her aunts take their usual seat in the front row on the right side of the courtroom.

Marlon, dressed in a dark blue suit with a shirt and tie, is led into the courtroom by an officer from a side entrance. Marlon sits at the defendant's table waiting for Leroy to join him.

The delay in Carolyn and Leroy's return gives Mary another opportunity to glare at the young man who killed her son. Her thoughts are not pleasant or compassionate.

Each day of the trial, when Marlon entered the courtroom, Mary would whisper to herself, "There's that animal...!" Looking at Marlon irritates her. She's disgusted. The trial has revived her hatred for him. On several occasions during the trial, she would tell her aunts how much she hated him.

Mary can't rationalize how a person so young can build up enough anger, in a matter of minutes, to shoot and kill someone – to kill her son. What makes a person do something so heartless? A myriad of thoughts run through Mary's mind as she looks at Marlon.

Marlon's head is down, occasionally looking up at the judge's empty seat. He makes a good decision to not look to his right. If he did, he would see a seething woman analyzing him.

An officer leads Carolyn and Leroy into the courtroom.

Carolyn takes her front row seat on the left side of the room directly behind the defendant's table. A wooden rail separates her from her son.

Moments later, Judge Christensen, the jury and prosecuting attorneys enter the courtroom. After some preliminary announcements by Judge Christensen, he asks the jury if they have reached a verdict.

A man acting as jury foreperson stands up and says, "Yes we have Your Honor."

Judge Christensen instructs Marlon to stand up. Leroy stands with him.

The foreperson gives a piece of paper to a court officer, who delivers it to Judge Christensen.

The Judge unfolds the paper and reads the verdict to himself. He then gives the paper to the court clerk and instructs her to read the verdict for all to hear.

"In the case of the State of Minnesota versus Marlon Rockshawn Green, we the jury find the defendant guilty of the charge of murder in the second degree."

On the day before his 18th birthday, Marlon is told he will be punished for his crime. His sentence is 25 ½ years. Downgrading the charge to second degree murder gives Marlon a chance for parole after 17 years based on good behavior. But most of Marlon's young adult life will be spent in prison.

Marlon shows no emotion after hearing his fate.

Carolyn bursts into tears, sobbing loudly. Leroy tries to console her.

Mary and her aunts grab each other's hands. Each of them uses the same words to describe their feelings, "Thank you Jesus…Thank you Jesus…Thank you Jesus!"

Mary watches Marlon being led away by a court officer. The look of vindication and anger on Mary's face is evident. An MRI exam would not find a single ounce of compassion for Marlon in her body. The justice system has granted Mary the hollow victory she was hoping for – hollow only in the sense that there is no reason for a celebration. Any joy in Mary's soul has been absent since Laramiun's death.

There is one consolation, however. Mary and her aunts no longer have to come to this courtroom to relive the painful memories of the crime and what led to the shooting. For that conclusion, Mary is grateful and relieved.

The same cannot be said for Carolyn. She's standing with her arms extended as if she will have a chance to hug Marlon.

The hug never happens.

Marlon goes through the side door of the courtroom. He's gone.

The verdict leaves two mothers with shattered dreams for their sons.

Carolyn continues to cry, saying Marlon's name over and over…

Members of Mary's Two Mothers organization showing
their unity after a meeting.

"

# THERE IS A NOBILITY IN COMPASSION, A BEAUTY IN EMPATHY, A GRACE IN FORGIVENESS.

— JOHN CONNOLLY

# CHAPTER SEVEN

## *Transformation for Mary and Marlon?*

There is no closure for Mary in the aftermath of the verdict. In the years following the trial, she wrestles with her anger, and occasionally, her faith. She doesn't sing gospel tunes around the house as much as she used to, but she still goes to church every Sunday and participates in weekly events at her church.

Mary was true to her Christian values before Laramiun's death and she's determined to keep that mindset, regardless of the painful moments she feels. She has been going to church since she was in the sixth grade. Her parents joined a church in North Minneapolis and made sure she came along. Her father became a deacon.

One of the reasons Mary enjoyed going to church was her passion for singing. She joined the youth choir and rarely missed performances when the choir was asked to sing during church service.

The lack of motivation to sing bothers Mary. Singing and talking to God in the morning always kept her in an upbeat mood. She still talks to God in the morning, but she would be the first to admit things are different with her. It takes a lot more to make her smile. She's not as sociable. Every now and then, she uses her solitude to ask herself if there was anything else she could have done, anything else she could have said to Laramiun to keep him safe. Laramiun was a confident, boastful young man. Mary wonders if she talked to him enough about being more humble. She still doesn't know all the circumstances that led to Laramiun's death. All she knows is that her son got into a beef at a party with a teen-ager he didn't know. Mary has conceded that she might never know what really happened, but the end result changed her life forever.

Pictures of Laramiun in Mary's living room remind her of his absence. She often picks up one of his photos and clutches it to her chest – the same way she would hold him when he was a baby. As she holds the photo, the word still comes out of her mouth... *Why?*

There is nothing special about Mary's grief. Mothers like her around the country experience the same heartache. It's almost a daily occurrence in our society when we hear of a mother losing her child to gun violence or some other criminal act. How do mothers hold on and survive after such a terrible experience? Where does the strength come from?

Mary's spirituality is tested whenever someone mentions what happened to Laramiun at the party. A look of discontent comes across her face. She doesn't hesitate to express the hatred she still feels for Marlon. "He's an animal," Mary often says.

That's the word she regularly used to describe the young man who killed her son. She felt that way about him during the trial and her feelings hadn't changed. What Mary doesn't know is that the "animal" is showing traces of maturity.

Two years into his prison sentence at St. Cloud (Minn.) Correctional Facility, the man the State of Minnesota referred to as Marlon Rockshawn Green is no longer using that name.

Marlon changes his name to Oshea Israel, following the lead of some older inmates who he saw reading the Bible every day. Marlon has taken time to read passages in the Old Testament and was influenced to make the change. He came across Genesis 32:28: "…Your name will no longer be Jacob, but Israel, because you have struggled with God and with humans and have overcome." (NIV)

More Old Testament reading led Marlon to a prophet named Hosea, also known as Hoshea, which means "deliverance." Marlon does some editing with the name and takes off the 'H', thus becoming Oshea. Marlon made the name change after his annual review in 1996.

Before establishing his new identity, he reached a significant milestone. Oshea earned his General Education Development (GED) certificate five months after entering prison. For a person who believed school was "boring," Oshea demonstrated a surprising and quick commitment to complete his high school education.

But the name change and GED are not previews of an accelerated rehabilitation for Oshea Israel. Oshea still considers himself "hard core" and resumes his gang activities while inside. There are rival gang members in the St. Cloud prison and Oshea still has allegiance to the Gangster Disciples. For safety reasons, it's important for Oshea to maintain a connection to his crew. Laramiun was promoting his affiliation with the Crips when he and Oshea got into it at the party. Oshea has to be alert whenever he knows Crips members are close by. He assumes an "organizer" role with the Gangster Disciples, which often leads to conflicts with guards and inmates. Despite his name change and GED achievement, Oshea still has the fearless demeanor of a criminal.

Six months after earning his GED, Oshea is given 45 days of segregation for assaulting an inmate. Segregation would become a familiar punishment for Oshea during the early years of his prison term.

*January 2004*

Mary is finishing up another work day at her church. She's been working full time as an administrative assistant at the church since US West closed her department in 1998. Mary had been with US West for 20 years.

The sudden end to a lengthy history with a company would be traumatic for some people. For Mary, it was a sign to move on and find a new calling with her life. She wasn't comfortable at US West during her last five years there. It was difficult at times to be in the office because of her memories of Laramiun. None of her co-workers will forget the day she found out about Laramiun while working at her desk. Mary never forgot either.

There is peace and solace for Mary in her new job. She's in church every day of the week and the work is rewarding. She has the satisfaction of providing assistance and services to congregation members, a role she embraces after her church was so supportive when Laramiun died.

Mary still has her community engagement instincts from her US West days. She had grown accustomed to interacting with people and didn't want that part of her life to change. After the trial, Mary searched for support groups that help mothers of slain children. She felt the need to belong to a group or organization to assist her in the healing process. Her search produces few options.

A referral from a court assistance program in Hennepin County led Mary to an organization where parents of slain children would come together to share their stories. Mary's involvement didn't last long. She heard parents talk about their situations, but she didn't see signs of healing or movement toward reconciliation – or solutions to help people get to that point. Healing and reconciliation were key elements for Mary in her search for help. She knew she needed some type of remedy to help her move on with her life. Mary felt this organization was standing in the same place, so she stopped attending their sessions.

The idea came to Mary to try to have her own group meetings. She advertised the meetings though neighborhood community agencies. She tried four times to have meetings for mothers like herself but no one came. Mary refused to give up. By now, she understood that this would be a developing mission for her, a revelation that started when she spoke to those young people at

Laramiun's memorial service. Mary knew there was an outlet somewhere for herself and similar mothers, and she was determined to find it.

Mary's pro-active nature eventually leads her to form her own organization – From Death To Life. The name was suggested by a close friend, Regina Irwin, a counselor in Minneapolis who works with women overcoming barriers and social issues. Regina, a devout Christian as well, told Mary one day about a Bible verse that resonated with Mary and made a lasting impact.

*"We know we have passed from death to life, because we love each other.*

*Anyone who does not love remains in death."* *– 1 John 3:14 (NIV)*

The verse becomes a key part of the work Mary hopes to do someday for mothers like herself. Mary's vision is to create an organization where mothers can come together and share their experiences of losing a child to violence. The idea is in the talking stages for Mary and Regina, who can relate to what Mary has been through. Regina's father was murdered at a house party in Minneapolis when she was 18. Her father and a man got into a fight, resulting in her father being hit with a piece of wood nearly the size of a baseball bat. The impact knocked her father through a nearby window.

Adding more hurt to Regina's family is that the assailant was not charged in the case. Regina's father was a boxer. His hands were licensed as a legal weapon. The assailant was able to make a strong case for self-defense. At least Mary was able to see a conviction for her son's killer. Regina and her family never got closure for what happened to her father. Regina's tragedy makes her a valuable ally for Mary. The two establish a permanent link that leads to life-changing moments for both of them.

Though Regina has given Mary the foundation for the name of her organization, Mary is not ready to move forward with her vision.

Eleven years had passed since Laramiun's death, but Mary continues to struggle with bitter feelings towards the man convicted of murdering her son. Her soul is still in conflict.

*January 26, 2004*

Oshea, now 27, walks out of a segregation cell at Stillwater (Minn.) Correctional Facility after a 15-day penalty for illegal use of a phone. All phone conversations for inmates are monitored. He made comments in the conversation that were ruled a violation. He was transferred to Stillwater in 1999 to finish out the rest of his sentence as an adult. He had a more serious phone violation in 2003 that led to 170 days in segregation.

Eighteen discipline reports had been filed against Oshea, including six major violations, since he entered prison in 1994. In one of the major violations, resulting in 105 days of segregation, he was serving food in the kitchen when he and an inmate came to blows. But on this particular morning, the end of Oshea's brief segregation turned out to be his last infraction.

Oshea had been showing signs of improving his behavior before the 15-day penalty.

He earned a certificate for completing a course in Critical Thinking Skills. Certificates were also handed to him for completing two training programs – one for Vocational Baking and the other to qualify as a Volunteer Basic Reading Tutor. Oshea helped organize a study group where inmates read books and discuss the topics and main storylines. He gives inmates "homework assignments" to make reports on what they read at the group's next meeting.

Reading had become a major activity for Oshea. Older inmates have encouraged him to spend more time in the library and he followed their advice. One inmate started ordering books for

Oshea. Two of the publications that catches his interest are Tavis Smiley's "Covenant With Black America" (Third World Press, 2006) and Robert Greene's "Art Of Seduction" (Penguin Publishing Group, 2001).

There's an interesting connection between Oshea and his prison mentors: all of them are incarcerated for murder. Some will remain in prison for the rest of their life. Isn't it amazing, and somewhat unfortunate, how prison walls can develop literary characteristics in a person who has committed violent acts? Perhaps the passion for reading and learning was always there. The frustrations of society simply got in the way.

It's obvious Oshea had the intelligence to be a successful student had he stayed in school and not dismissed the value of an education. Taking a leadership role in the study group and reading thought-provoking novels in the prison library prove that he had an untapped intellect before the house party. It was evident in his love for rap music, which essentially is poetry set to rhythmic beats.

Before his conviction, Oshea spent a lot of his spare time writing lyrics for rap songs and studying his favorite rap artists. The rap/hip-hop culture often gets criticized for its lyrics and questionable images, but all of the industry's stars had to be able to read and write to build successful careers. He was following the footsteps of the rappers he idolized, capturing the elements of the world they live in while putting the words and thoughts to music.

The encouragement Oshea was getting from fellow inmates to expand his thinking and knowledge is coming at the right time for him. He's fed up with all the segregation penalties, the fighting and gang activities. He has developed a particular interest in empowering African-American inmates. It hit home one day for Oshea that he's in prison for what he did to an African-American man. Black-on-black crime is not a term he was focused on before his fatal confrontation with Laramiun. It's on his radar now, and he's determined to make peace with himself for what he'd done.

The hard-core persona Oshea displayed when he entered prison is shifting toward compassion and understanding. He is no longer an angry teen-ager. He has become a man who wants to prove he can make positive contributions inside and outside of the correctional system. Oshea has no idea that this surging transformation is leading him to another life-changing moment.

*January 26, 2004*

Mary settles onto her living room couch with a dinner plate and turns the TV to one of her favorite channels, the Trinity Broadcast Network. Mary likes the religious-based programming on TBN and regularly makes time to watch the channel. She's unsure of what's on tonight, but she plans to watch anyway.

Mary sees the name R.T. Kendall flash on the bottom of the screen. The host of the program is interviewing Kendall, a prominent minister in England and well-known author. Mary is not familiar with Kendall but the subject of the interview immediately catches her attention.

Kendall is answering questions about his latest book and quotes a few paragraphs.

Mary focuses in on the conversation. She stops eating and puts down her fork.

Kendall's comments are eerily similar to things Mary has been casually thinking about lately.

Mary puts her plate aside and gets up to find a pen and paper. As the interview draws to a close, the name of Kendall's book and how to purchase it is displayed on the screen. Mary writes down Kendall's name and the book title.

She doesn't realize the show has ended and the network has gone to a commercial break. She's holding the scratch sheet of paper in her hand and staring at the title of Kendall's book….

*"Total Forgiveness."*

Mary meets President Obama during a visit to Minneapolis when he was in office.

Forgiveness is an act of the will, and the will can function regardless of the temperature of the heart."
- Corrie ten Boom

# CHAPTER EIGHT

### *'I want to meet my son's killer'*

Two days after seeing R.T. Kendall talk about his "Total Forgiveness" (Charisma House, 2002) book on TV, Mary goes to a bookstore to buy it. She finishes the 185-page book in three days. She is captivated by Kendall's teachings and philosophy, much of it based on the Bible, which makes her even more impressionable.

There are numerous passages, motivations, recommendations and directives that intrigue Mary, making her wonder if her heart and spirit is truly in the right place when she thinks about Laramiun's death and the man responsible.

Some of the passages in Kendall's book tug at Mary...

*"The greater the sin you must forgive, the greater measure of the Spirit that will come to you..."*

*"Welcome the opportunity to forgive the deepest hurt, the greatest injustice, and remember that a greater anointing is waiting for you..."*

*"Examine your motives and be sure you aren't doing it to punish anyone by making them look bad..."*

If Mary is seriously trying to rationalize in her heart whether she can forgive Marlon, she will have to consider that last passage first. Why would she do it? Is she only thinking about it to get back at Marlon in some way? The soul-searching process appears to be underway in Mary, but she's nowhere near making the decision to pursue such a vision.

Mary is enlightened enough by Kendall's book to share the findings with her pastor.

The day after she finished reading the book, Mary brings it to work, shows it to her pastor, and had a revealing conversation with him. She is so adept at explaining the book's concepts, she unknowingly talks herself into an assignment.

The pastor asks Mary to teach a Sunday school class about forgiveness, using Kendall's book as the framework for a lesson plan. Mary has an 'Are-you-serious-look?' on her face. Her pastor just presented her with an opportunity to teach something she's been stressing about for 11 years. How can this be?

The answer is simple: This is one of those examples of how the Lord works in mysterious ways to get things done. It doesn't sink in with Mary right away, but getting the opportunity to teach this forgiveness class is one of those moments that will make sense later.

This Sunday school class is not for kids or teenagers. Mary's lesson plan will be aimed at adults who are wise enough to form their own opinions and challenge Mary to see if she really knows what she's talking about. Even more critical for Mary in her teaching role is whether she can prove to a room full of adults that she really believes in her message of forgiveness. That's the part that worries Mary the most. She has yet to demonstrate her own spirit of forgiveness, so how will she be able to serve as an effective teacher – or better yet, an effective role model?

Mary decides to go through with it. For the next eight Sundays, she uses a different chapter in the book each week for her topic. Class size is 10-15 adults each week, including her dear friend Annette, who attends every Sunday as a show of support for Mary.

The challenge Mary feared surfaces one Sunday when the subject deals with "Forgiving God." Mary struggles with this lesson because she knows she has been angry about Laramiun's death and wondered why God allowed it to happen. She can see people in the class not believing her when she says she has "forgiven God." The push-back from some class members is another sign for Mary to do something about her conflict.

Mary gets an even stronger message the following Sunday when the next chapter – "The Lord's Prayer And Forgiveness" – touches a nerve and perhaps her soul. A key passage in the chapter seems to speak to her. She gets emotional and fights back tears when reading it to the class:

*"Making a choice to continue in unforgiveness shows that we aren't sufficiently grateful for God's forgiveness of our sins…"*

The one thing Mary never wanted, even in the depths of her grief over Laramiun, is to lose favor in the eyes of her Lord and Savior. Mary begins to understand that the assignment to teach this class is part of a Master Plan.

If it means doing the unthinkable or the unimaginable, she seems more receptive and curious about this phenomenon called forgiveness. Seeing Kendall on TV that night and getting the opportunity to teach this class cannot be considered a coincidence for Mary. A divine power is at work here, and Mary is beginning to feel the effects.

A couple of months after concluding her Sunday school class assignment, Mary participates in a prayer walk in North Minneapolis to help bring attention to the rising crime rate. Gang shootings are becoming more frequent and occasionally catch innocent bystanders in the crossfire. The beleaguered community is no different from most inner city African-American neighborhoods around the country, where gangs and crime are primary concerns.

Mary has kept her pulse on these types of community events, mainly because of Laramiun and her willingness to show support for mothers who lost children to violence. Whenever there is a rally or event designed to stand up against crime, Mary is there.

Near the end of the walk, Mary is walking alongside a woman who introduces herself.

"Hi! How are you? I'm Michelle Braley."

"Mary Johnson. Nice to meet you!"

Michelle tells Mary she's a social worker at an organization on West Broadway. As the walk comes to an end, Michelle asks Mary about her connection to the walk.

"I'm out here to show support for the people who have lost family members to violence, particularly the mothers who have lost kids," Mary says. "I lost my son 11 years ago."

"Sorry to hear that. What happened if you don't mind me asking?"

"My son was at a party. A man shot and killed him. They got the guy. He's in prison."

"Do you know which one?"

"Stillwater."

"I have a real close friend who works for the DOC (Minnesota Department of Corrections). He does what they call restorative justice. He does a lot of case work at Stillwater."

"I'm not familiar with that term…"

"Restorative justice is a program where they try to get offenders and victims of their crimes to come together for healing, or at least to communicate about the crime. Sometimes it works. Sometimes it doesn't…Depends on the circumstances."

Mary and Michelle continue to chat. The more they converse about this thing called "restorative justice," the more Mary is intrigued. Michelle can sense Mary's curiosity and suggests that she meet her friend, Tim Hansen, who coordinates the DOC's restorative justice program. Michelle tells Mary she's facilitating a community meeting in North Minneapolis in a few weeks and would like Mary to attend. Michelle says that Tim will be at the meeting and it would be a good opportunity for her to meet him.

Mary and Michelle exchange goodbyes after the prayer walk.

As Michelle walks away, Mary stands there for a moment, thinking about what just happened. First, the Sunday school class, then this chance meeting with a lady talking about something she has never heard of. Two words are implanted in Mary's memory as she tries to process her conversation with Michelle about restorative justice – victims and offenders. Both of those words have a chilling connection to Mary. Is there really a meaningful way to bring these two sides together? Even if attempts fail to put victim and offender in the same room for healing, the two sides will be linked forever by the crime committed.

Mary hasn't seen Marlon or had any communication with him since the trial ended. It still doesn't change the fact that they will have an ever-lasting link. Judging by recent events, Mary seems to be getting a spiritual nudge to learn more about the victim-offender dynamics.

*Three weeks later*

Michelle is close to wrapping up the Saturday afternoon community meeting she's facilitating. As she makes her final comments, she scans the audience and sees Mary on one side of the room and Tim on the other. Mary and Tim have not met, but Michelle is ready to change that as soon as she closes the meeting.

After shaking hands with a few people and saying goodbyes, Tim approaches Michelle and gives her a hug. They have been friends since the late 1980s when they worked for the Lutheran Volunteer Corps, an organization that places staff in various cities to learn about social justice. Tim and Michelle share similar passions about social justice and healing on both sides of the legal system.

Mary sees the greeting between the two and assumes the gentleman must be Tim.

Mary approaches, giving Michelle the opportunity to make the introduction, "Hi Mary! So glad you were able to come."

"Thanks for the invitation."

"Mary, this is Tim Hansen, the gentleman I've been telling you about."

Tim smiles and extends his hand to Mary. "Hello Mary! So nice to meet you. Michelle has told me about you and your situation. Sorry to hear about your son."

"Thank you."

Michelle leaves Tim and Mary so she can say goodbye to a few people.

Her exit gives Tim and Mary a chance to talk before Michelle returns. Tim and Mary sit down at a nearby table.

Tim gives Mary a general explanation of his role with the DOC. He identifies his position as a "planner" for the DOC's Restorative Justice Unit, a position he's worked with since 2000. He was a psychology major at Winona State (Minn.) and has spent most of his professional career working for transitional programs with organizations in Minnesota, Washington state and Wisconsin.

Tim informs Mary that he helps plan something called "Victim Offender Dialogues (VOD)," sessions that are initiated by victims of crimes who have an interest in talking to or meeting the offender. Tim stresses to Mary that this is only considered when victims or their families make the request. Offenders are prohibited from seeking a VOD. It's one of the reasons why Tim is happy to hear of Mary's potential interest in pursuing one with Marlon. Raising more anticipation is the fact that Mary and Marlon would represent the first VOD at Stillwater. Tim quizzes Mary about her curiosity in talking with the man who killed her son. A victim's motive and purpose are key factors in determining whether a VOD is approved.

Michelle and Tim have made previous plans for dinner after the community meeting, forcing Tim to wrap up the conversation when Michelle returns. He gives Mary his business card and asks her to call him Monday morning to set up a meeting.

As Tim and Michelle leave the room, Mary has another one of those pensive moments. She stands there looking at Tim's card. More thoughts race through her mind. Things keep happening. She keeps meeting people connected to her dilemma. Whatever is going on, Mary hasn't shut it down. Her curiosity is outweighing any notion that all of this is just a coincidence. The term *restorative justice* has been planted in her mind and it's driving her to find out more.

The following week Tim comes to Mary's church to talk more extensively about his role and the restorative justice process. Mary is prepared with more questions. She has written down some notes to make sure she doesn't forget to ask Tim specific questions.

Tim can see in Mary's eyes that her curiosity is sincere.

Mary tells Tim about the forgiveness class she taught in Sunday school at her church and how it gave her the idea about meeting the man who caused her so much pain. She explains that she needs to find out if she has forgiven him, and in her mind, the only way to answer that question is to meet him face-to-face, on his turf.

After talking for about an hour and a half, Tim asks Mary, "Well, what do you think?"

Mary pauses a moment and glances at a picture of Laramiun on her desk. The smile on her face fades, replaced by an expression of determination as she looks at her son. She looks at Tim before answering his question. "I want to do this," Mary says with soft conviction. "I want to meet my son's killer."

Tim nods his head in support. He's happy to hear that she wants to make the attempt, but he cautions her about the process and the many steps involved before the meeting can take place. "Mary, you'll have to show patience and persistence to get through the process," Tim says. "Sometimes it's not easy. There will be hurdles and sometimes setbacks. Your commitment in this is crucial."

"I'm ready," Mary responds without hesitation,

After Tim leaves the church, Mary returns to her office and looks at Laramiun's picture again on her desk. Her heart seems to be doing the talking, as if she's letting Laramiun know that she's moving closer to reconciliation over what happened to him. The meeting with Tim solidified Mary's interest to pursue her true feelings about Marlon, and more importantly, true feelings within herself.

If Mary gets an opportunity to teach more lessons on forgiveness at her church, she knows she can't take on the assignment without fully embracing the concept. She has to walk it before she can preach it. At the moment, she has already taken a few steps toward her goal.

Tim's first priority is to do some research on Marlon. He wants to find out about his character and check his discipline file. Tim wants to be sure that Marlon meets the requirements of an inmate who's willing to participate in a VOD. He notices his name change to Oshea and that he has improved his education and behavior over the past two years.

Satisfied with the improvement in Oshea's behavior, Tim sets up a meeting with him. Looking at a file is one thing. Tim wants to see for himself what kind of guy Oshea is and make his own determination. Tim goes to Stillwater to meet him but instructs the staff to not tell Oshea what the meeting is about. Oshea has never heard of Tim and has no idea why he's been summoned to meet with him.

Tim begins the meeting asking Oshea about his case, then describes restorative justice to him. He tells Oshea that someone wants to meet him in relation to his case. Tim doesn't say who until later in the conversation. When Tim feels it's appropriate, he informs Oshea that Mary Johnson, the mother of the man he shot and killed at the party, is the person who wants to meet him.

Oshea is cautious with his response. He tells Tim he wants to take some time to think about it. He mentions to Tim that one reason he's not sure about meeting with Mary is his concern for possible retaliation. Oshea is wondering if this is about revenge for him or his family, or if the meeting with Mary could be some type of setup.

In spite of Oshea's hesitation, Tim is not discouraged. He still believes Oshea is a good candidate for a VOD, but he has to give his consent. A meeting with Mary is totally up to him. Tim explains to Oshea that he is not obligated, but Oshea assures him that he will think about it.

Tim shakes Oshea's hand and thanks him for his time.

Later in the day, Tim calls Mary to tell her how the meeting went, and that Oshea will let him know about his decision.

A week goes by. Tim gets a message from a Stillwater staff member. Oshea says no.

Oshea told his inner circle of inmates about Mary's inquiry. All of them said he should meet with her, but he resists.

"What she want to talk to me about?" Oshea asked his mentors. "I really don't have anything to say to her."

Though Oshea is more mature now, the thought of sitting down with Mary brings back memories of the shooting. For everyone involved, the shooting would be imbedded in their memories forever, but Oshea has done a creditable job of moving past the crime and making strides toward rehabilitation. He is not the same person who fired the gun that night, yet he's not particularly interested in going down memory lane with the mother of the man he killed. Oshea is thinking 'what purpose will it serve'? The meeting won't reduce his sentence. It won't even lead to more privileges in the prison.

Oshea found it hard to find positives for sitting down with Mary. He would just rather continue serving his time with as few setbacks as possible. In about five years, he will eligible to be released. He doesn't want anything to get in the way of that, especially a meeting with Mary. So many things can trigger behavior relapses for inmates regardless of their mental toughness. Oshea is very confident with his state of mind, knowing that his release is within sight. A meeting with Mary just isn't in his best interest right now.

Tim dreads making the call to Mary to inform her of Oshea's decision. He knows how important this mission is to her.

Tim tells Mary that Oshea declined to meet with her.

"He's got a lot of nerve," an irritated Mary says.

Tim lets Mary know that he will continue to make the effort to set up the meeting. Mary is not optimistic. She calls Annette to tell her the news that Marlon said no to her meeting request. Mary has kept Annette updated on what she's trying to do. One of the reasons Mary wants to meet with him is to ask him why he shot Laramiun. Victim-offender dialogues are designed to get everything out in the open regarding the crime. For some offenders, going back to that moment might be too stressful. At this point, Mary is unsure if she will have the opportunity to get answers from him.

A few days after Oshea declines, Tim tries another approach. He asks Sherlinda Wheeler, a female African-American case worker at Stillwater, for her assistance. Tim is thinking that Sherlinda's bubbly, yet forceful personality might sway Oshea to change his mind. Sherlinda has a good rapport with many of the inmates but isn't as familiar with Oshea.

Before approaching Oshea, she looks into his file. She sees the same improvement as Tim did when he checked on Oshea. If his file has too many recent discipline reports, Sherlinda would not recommend him for a VOD.

Sherlinda makes a note to herself to talk to Oshea during lunch hour. She goes to the kitchen where he is working as a food server. She tells him to stop what he's doing and come into the hallway.

Oshea glares at Sherlinda. He wonders what he has done to make her interrupt his job duties.

"I heard about you saying you don't want to meet with Mary Johnson," Sherlinda says in a stern voice. "I'm here to tell you you're gonna meet with her. Stop playing around. You need to do this."

"Okay, okay, I'll do it," Oshea says. "Don't be so hard on me!" Oshea flashes a quick grin.

"Thank you!" Sherlinda says firmly. "Get back to work." Sherlinda walks to her office with a smile on her face. She knows Stillwater has had difficulty setting up VOD sessions. She thinks she just made a breakthrough by getting a commitment from Oshea.

What changed? In a matter of days, Oshea agrees to meet with Mary. Sherlinda's "persuasive demand" is a key factor, but older inmates have been in Oshea's ear recently telling him he should meet with Mary. By the time Sherlinda stormed into the kitchen to tell Oshea what to do, he had already been thinking about changing his mind. Oshea has realized there's a part of himself in need of reconciliation. All the reading he's been doing in recent years has helped make him more open-minded about his life when he leaves prison and what he did at that house party. Like Mary, the time for healing and understanding appears to be tugging at him as well.

When Sherlinda gets to her office, she immediately calls Tim to break the news to him. Tim is excited. He thanks Sherlinda for her help and calls Mary. Getting Oshea to agree to a meeting is a major development for the prison and the efforts to coordinate VOD sessions.

"Wow, that's wonderful," Mary says to Tim.

Mary and Tim talk for a few more minutes. Tim gives her instructions on the next steps in the process and sets up another meeting for the two of them. When Mary hangs up the phone, she has a look of uncertainty on her face. What she's been thinking about, what she's been asking for, is about to become a reality. The process is officially in motion for Mary to meet her son's killer and determine if she understands the true meaning of forgiveness.

Mary almost forgets to call Annette to tell her the good news.

"Girl, he wants to meet! Can you believe it?"

Excited for her friend, Annette has a simple response for Mary, "That's God making a way for you!"

*July 2004*

A lot has to be done before a date is set for Mary and Oshea to meet. Tim enlists Michelle to help him facilitate a series of meetings with Mary. They will also meet several times with Oshea at Stillwater. Mary and Oshea must undergo intensive questioning and interviewing to help them prepare for their meeting, which is not guaranteed. At any point in the process, Mary or Oshea could change their minds and say they don't want to do it. But a meeting wouldn't be scheduled until Tim and Michelle feel Mary and Oshea were ready.

Since Mary has to be the initiator in this process, her motives and expectations must be clear. She has to convince Tim, Michelle and the DOC that she's not pursuing this out of revenge or an attempt to make Oshea feel bad. She tells Tim and Michelle that she has three main reasons for wanting to meet with Oshea: Why did he kill Laramiun? Why did he change his name? Can I forgive him?

Tim advises Mary to have a support person by her side as she prepares to meet Oshea. Regina is the first person who comes to mind.

Regina, very familiar with Mary's situation, agrees to help her friend. She has some early advice for Mary. "Remember, the person you're trying to meet is no longer a 16 year old boy," she tells Mary. "He's a grown man now."

Oshea appears to be making satisfactory progress toward rehabilitation. He's up for parole in 2010. If he earns his release, he'll be on probation until August 2018. This is a critical time for him. How he handles the preparation process for the VOD could have long-term implications on his potential release.

As part of the preparation, Tim recommends to Mary and Regina that they participate in a 10-week program at Shakopee (Minn.) Prison, a female correctional facility about 35 miles south of Minneapolis. The program is called Victims Offenders Community: A Restorative Experience, more commonly known as VOCARE.

VOCARE is a Latin term that means "to call, to summons, invoke, invite or to gather." The Minnesota DOC is embracing the VOCARE principle to bring together people harmed by a crime and offenders who committed the crime. The group sessions also include community members with no personal connection to the criminal act. The intent is to coordinate these sessions in front of a neutral, small group of people who are allowed to observe a potential healing in a personal way. It's a unique approach to addressing the causes and consequences of a crime.

Tim believes the VOCARE is a vital step for Mary in her preparation to meet with Oshea.

Everyone attending VOCARE sessions sits in a circle to listen to offenders and victims share their stories. The ultimate objective is reconciliation – and healing. Tim wants Mary to have an up-close experience in watching offenders express their feelings. The hope is that Mary's views of Oshea, particularly her past remarks of calling him an "animal," will soften after witnessing a human element among offenders. Though this VOCARE is scheduled at a women's facility, Tim is confident the impact will be the same.

Mary is skeptical of the VOCARE sessions, but she and Regina make the commitment to participate. All of the sessions are on Monday nights. After attending the first session, Mary and Regina are unsure if they would return. A woman whose son was murdered by his girlfriend shared her son's story with the group and showed pictures of him, but Mary is surprised the woman made no reference to the offender. That's what Mary was waiting for. The woman's story about her son is the only story the group heard.

The VOCARE program is off to a slow start for Mary and Regina, but both know if they don't come back, it could jeopardize Mary's attempts to meet with Oshea. They return next week to honor their commitment. What happens the second week leaves a lasting impression on Mary. An offender involved in a murder as an accomplice stands in the circle and begins to tell her story. She knows the victim and victim's family are not in the circle. When she mentions that the victim and their family are not present, she gets emotional and starts to cry. She's distraught that she's not able to apologize to the family for her role in the crime. She wants to ask for forgiveness.

The room is quiet. Everyone feels compassion for the young woman. As the woman tries to compose herself to continue, Mary breaks the silence: "Pretend I'm the mother...You can apologize to me."

Something was triggered inside Mary to become an active participant in this session. When Tim recommended the VOCARE program to Mary, he never told her that she had to be vocal. All Mary had to do is listen and observe. Just being in the room would give her a perspective on the victim-offender dynamics. Mary, however, has been moved by the woman's attempts to apologize and inserts herself into this dramatic moment.

The woman, initially startled by Mary's offer, walks toward Mary and stands about five feet in front of her. The woman locks eyes with Mary and tearfully explains her role in the crime and what happened. She begins to make her apology. When she concludes, she clasps her hands together as if she's praying and says to Mary, "Ma'am, I am so sorry. Would you please forgive me?"

Mary's eyes fill with tears before the woman asks for forgiveness. The powerful testimony is affecting her. As she listened to the woman's story, she's wondering how to process this moment, wondering if this is what it's all about. A quick flashback pops up in Mary's mind. She sees Oshea shooting Laramiun at the party.

Mary blinks her eyes, returning her attention to the woman. She responds, "Yes, I do…I forgive you." She stands up and gives the woman a long hug. Both of the ladies are crying, and everyone else in the room is wiping their eyes, including Regina.

The emotional moment changes Mary. She realizes that criminals are human beings like the rest of us. Though the woman has lost her freedom because of the crime, Mary felt compassion for her. Mary has a clearer understanding of her mission, and perhaps a different view of the man she had been calling an "animal."

In a women's prison, a major breakthrough occurs for Mary in her search for forgiveness. Mary and Regina attend the next eight sessions to complete the program. Mary's willingness to play the role of a victim's mother, a role she needed no rehearsal for, might have saved her mission to meet with Oshea. The meeting is still within reach after Mary and Regina finished a key step in the process.

*Early March 2005*

Mary is working at her church when she gets a call from Tim. It's the call she's been waiting for since Oshea changed his mind and agreed to meet with her. Tim tells Mary that her meeting with Oshea is set for Saturday, March 26th. The date is about three weeks away, but Mary is relieved to finally know when she'll have the chance to confront the man who took the life of her only child. She marks the date on her calendar and begins a personal countdown. There is no turning back now.

*Sunday, March 20, 2005*

Mary feels a critical need to be in church this morning. It's the final Sunday before her meeting on Saturday with Oshea. Mary wants as much spiritual momentum as she can muster to get ready. She didn't wait until today. Mary started a 21-day fast the day after she received the call from Tim to confirm the date and time for the meeting. All Mary has eaten or drank the past three weeks is vegetables, water and V8 juice. She plans to end her fast after today's church service. Mary hopes she has fulfilled a large part of her personal game plan to be mentally ready for the meeting.

Though Mary is not in the church choir, she has been singing with more enthusiasm in recent weeks with the congregation. Her push to unlock the mystery of forgiveness has re-charged her spiritual strength and brought her closer to one of her passions. Singing in church has been one of her traditions for years and she seems happy with the re-connection. On this particular Sunday morning, Mary's voice and hand-clapping is more firm and confident. She's in a good place emotionally, although her state of mind is about to make an interesting turn.

After the choir finishes a song, the pastor and his wife tell the congregation they would like to do a special prayer for the mothers who have sons. In the wake of rising crime rates and gun violence in African-American communities in Minneapolis and surrounding areas, the couple is compelled to bring mothers to the altar to help pray for the safety of their sons.

About a dozen women make their way to the altar to receive prayers from the pastor and his wife.

As the pastor and his wife offer individual prayers to each woman, Mary's spirit is twitching. Something is tugging at her to go up to the altar and join the women. How can this be? Mary's son is gone.

Mary is used to hearing a "voice" speak to her, or in her words, the voice of the Holy Spirit that's attempting to deliver her a message. She heard that voice in her sister Mildred's bathroom when she learned Laramiun was dead.

*"I've done what you asked me to do. I have him…"*

The Holy Spirit is trying to get her attention this morning. Just before the pastor and his wife conclude their prayers for the last woman at the altar, Mary feels the urge to stand up. She walks toward the altar as the last woman returns to her seat. Mary is at the altar alone with the pastor and his wife. She can't help but wonder if people in the congregation are thinking she's finally lost it. The stress of losing Laramiun and this quest for forgiveness has pushed her over the edge, made her lose touch with reality. Has the time come for Mary to seek medical help?

What Mary is seeking at this moment is guidance. She truly believes she belongs at the altar – even if the entire congregation is aware that her son is gone. Mary is asking God to lay His comforting hands on Oshea and Carolyn, the mother who still has her son, the mother who Mary was ready to fight in the lobby outside that courtroom all those years ago. Mary is asking for blessings for Oshea, the man she used to call an animal.

When the pastor and his wife set aside time to pray for mothers with sons, Mary stands in for Carolyn and Oshea at the altar. Is Mary's path to forgiveness already underway? This is the second time Mary has shown signs of a major turnaround with her feelings.

At Shakopee Prison, she was moved enough to stand in and play a victim's mother.

Is Mary capable of asserting herself one more time?

Mary and Sister Mary Margaret McKenzie of the Visitation Sisters of Minneapolis.

FORGIVENESS DOESN'T
EXCUSE THEIR BEHAVIOR.

FORGIVENESS PREVENTS
THEIR BEHAVIOR FROM
DESTROYING YOUR HEART.

#BEYONDORDINARY

# CHAPTER NINE

### *The Meeting – Will Forgiveness Be Finalized?*

*Friday night, March 25, 2005*

Mary and Regina pull up to the hotel in Stillwater, Minn., smiling and laughing during their upbeat conversation. As they get out of the car, their hands are full with plastic bags. They just returned from a shopping spree at a nearby mall in Stillwater. Both saw too many items they didn't want to leave in the stores.

Shopping and dinner at the mall is good therapy for Mary. She didn't make one mention of her agenda tomorrow morning or the real reason they're in Stillwater. That's exactly the way Regina wants the evening to go. It was Regina's plan to spend a festive evening with Mary to keep Mary's mind off tomorrow.

When Mary and Regina learned of the meeting date with Oshea, they made plans to go to Stillwater the day before to avoid making the long drive early in the morning. Stillwater is almost an hour drive from North Minneapolis and with the meeting scheduled for 10 a.m., Mary and Regina didn't want to take any chances of being late or rushing to get to the prison.

The DOC offered to pay the one-night hotel stay for Mary and Regina, giving them a chance to arrive a day early and have breakfast tomorrow morning with Tim and Michelle. It would be one more opportunity for Mary to talk with Tim and Michelle before the meeting.

After Mary and Regina unload their shopping bags in the hotel room, Regina connects her portable DVD player to the TV. Regina brought along her DVD player, so Mary could watch a movie later tonight. Regina wants Mary to watch "Shawshank Redemption," a popular prison film released in 1994. The film earned an Oscar nominee for Best Picture.

Regina hasn't missed a beat in her role to get Mary ready for tomorrow. The rationale for watching the movie is to give Mary a better idea of prison life. Tomorrow's meeting will be Mary's first venture inside a male correctional facility.

Before Regina inserts the movie, she asks Mary to join her in a prayer. They kneel at the side of one of the double beds. Near the end of the prayer session, Regina asks the Lord to give Mary "strength and resolve as she heads into a pivotal moment in her life." After both say "Amen," they help each other up.

Mary doesn't let go of Regina's arm and gives her a quick hug. "Thank you."

"You're welcome. Now watch this movie!"

Mary smiles and shakes her head in playful disgust. "You're just determined to make me watch this aren't you?"

Regina nods at her. "Yes, I am." Regina inserts the disc, pushes the play button and walks away from the TV to get ready for bed. She has seen the film before and has no plans of staying up to watch it with her friend.

Several minutes into the film, Regina falls asleep, but Mary remains wide awake in her bed. She watches the entire two-hour, 20-minute film, making mental notes to discuss with Regina in the morning. Regina's plan worked. Shawshank Redemption put some things into Mary's mind.

*Saturday morning, March 26, 2005*

Mary and Regina have been up since 6:30. It's almost 7:30 and Mary hasn't said anything to Regina about the movie. Regina hasn't asked. She's testing her friend to see if Mary will bring up the subject.

Mary has been busy packing her things and getting dressed, perhaps the perfect excuse to avoid talking about the movie. The TV is another outlet for Mary. She and Regina have been watching the morning news. A couple of news stories prompt Mary and Regina to give their own "news analysis" about what's going on in the world as they stand in front of the mirror applying finishing touches on their hair and makeup.

Tired of the idle chit-chat, Regina pops the question, "So, what did you think about the movie?"

Mary continues to comb her hair – then makes a slight sound of disgust in her voice as she answers, "Girl, that movie had me crying a couple of times. I watched it all 'til the end. It's so sad what those guys have to go through sometimes when they're in there. I don't know if I can watch it again."

Regina nods. "That's okay. At least you have a sense of what you're about to see."

"Yeah, I know."

Mary and Regina pack up all their belongings and leave their hotel room to meet Tim and Michelle for breakfast.

Tim and Michelle want to do a final checkup on Mary to see how she's feeling about her mission and to observe any potential signs of hesitation or concern.

Mary gives no indication during the breakfast of cancelling. She knows if she scraps the meeting now, it will be a major disappointment to Tim, Michelle, Regina and others in the DOC who have worked hard to make this meeting happen. Mary reassures Tim and Michelle that she's ready.

The breakfast continues with casual and light-hearted conversation – until Tim looks at his watch. "We better get going," he says.

Tim's comment becomes a reality-check moment for Mary. Though she has given indications of being mentally ready for the meeting, Tim's time-to-go announcement ignites uneasy feelings. Mary realizes the conclusion of this breakfast officially begins the final steps toward her mission. The uncertainty of the outcome is creeping into her thoughts as she walks out of the restaurant with Regina, Tim and Michelle. She walks in silence. Her conscious, however, is in a very talkative mood.

What if Oshea still believes he's being set up and doesn't say much in the meeting? Fear of a setup is one of the reasons that he turned down Mary's first request. What if Mary's hatred and bitterness resurface as soon as she sees Oshea? How will she handle her first face-to-face encounter with the man who murdered her son? An explosive reaction from Mary could ruin months of preparation and quickly terminate the meeting. All of these thoughts nag at Mary while she walks to the car with Regina.

Tim and Michelle are in another car.

Mary and Regina follow them for the short ride to Stillwater Correctional Facility. Mary and Regina chat on the way, but when they turn into the visitors' parking lot, silence interrupts the conversation. The mood becomes somber for both.

Mary stares at the high walls of the main building and the nearby high fences topped with barbed wire. The walls are dark brown, lifeless – no signs, images or decorations. The outer image of Stillwater is like most prisons. There is no need to advertise the location or spruce up the landscape. It is not a happy destination, not even for visitors.

"This is such a sad place," Mary says softly. "Why would men do things to put them in a place like this?"

"Girl, only God knows the answer to that," Regina says.

Oshea is finishing up his breakfast in the dining hall. Inmates seated near him are having fun conversations about sports, challenging each other on their knowledge. Laughter breaks out when an inmate tries to sound authoritative.

Oshea is oblivious to the barber shop chatter. His mind is on the meeting he's about to have with the mother of the man he killed 12 years ago. Up until this point, Oshea has done everything asked of him during the preparation process. He passed every measuring point and was open and honest with all of his responses.

But the day has arrived. Oshea isn't nervous or anxious – just wondering and thinking. He's had meetings in prison many times but none like this. He looks over at the inmates nearby after hearing part of the conversation. He laughs with them. For Oshea, it's a very timely moment of comic relief.

Regina turns the ignition off, drops the keys in her purse, looks at Mary and proclaims, "Let's do this!"

As soon as Regina comes from the other side of the car, she grabs Mary's left hand for their walk through the parking lot. She feels Mary squeeze it. They walk toward the building in silence. When they get to the ramp leading to the main entrance, Regina drops Mary's hand and walks in front of her.

Regina takes a few steps before noticing that Mary has stopped walking.

"Girl, I don't think I can do this," Mary moans to Regina. A tear is trickling down her face.

Regina goes back to her friend and gets behind her to give her a gentle push up the ramp. "Mary, you said you wanted to do this because of other mothers...You're going to do this. You didn't come this far to back away now." Regina continues to push Mary up the ramp until they get to the main entrance. Regina can feel that Mary doesn't have the energy to make it through the door. She holds onto her as they enter the lobby area to get checked in.

Mary sees a women's bathroom to the left. "I need to go in there."

"Ok. I'll be right here."

Mary is in the bathroom for several minutes. Regina, sitting in the lobby, glances twice at the bathroom door but resists getting up to check on her friend. Regina knows that a bathroom often serves an additional purpose for Mary.

No matter where a bathroom is located, in Mary's mind, it's a sanctuary for her to talk to God.

More than ever, on this morning, Mary needs to have a conversation with God to give her strength to handle what she's about to go through. She almost didn't make it up the ramp outside. It's way too early for Mary to break down and she knows it.

Mary looks into the mirror, wiping tears away from under her eyes.

"Father, I know you didn't bring me this far for me to get weak all of a sudden. I know you haven't done that, but why am I so scared? Help me to keep in my spirit what you always tell me…That you never place things before us that we can't handle. If things do get rough for us, you always say *'Give your burdens to Me and walk with Me'*. Well, Father, walk with me today…"

Mary understands she can't have an extended talk with God, but she says enough to regain her composure. She dabs at her eyes one more time and walks out of the bathroom to rejoin Regina in the lobby.

Regina is smiling at Mary as she walks toward her. "You okay?" she asks in a comforting tone.

"Yeah, I'm all right…Just needed to have a conversation."

Tim and Michelle also give comforting looks to Mary. Tim puts his hand on Mary's shoulder.

Michelle gently grabs one of Mary's hands. "It's okay Mary. We'll all be with you the entire time."

Mary and Regina move toward the desk where a security officer is seated.

The officer tells them they will have to leave all of their possessions in a locker before going through the first set of heavy steel doors. Everything has to be placed in the locker.

"You mean I can't take my Bible in there?" Mary asks.

"Sorry Ma'am," the officer says.

Mary also has to leave behind a folder she is carrying with pictures of Laramiun. She was hoping to show Oshea pictures of her son when he was a child and a young adult. Mary is agitated. Her purse has been placed inside the locker. Inside her purse is a tube of lotion that she didn't get a chance to use when she came out of the bathroom.

Mary and Regina, as well as Tim and Michelle, are empty-handed when they go through the two sets of doors that lead into the secured areas and cell blocks. They don't have to walk far. The meeting room is only several feet past the checkpoint.

Mary's agitation continues as she and Regina stand outside the room. "Nothing's going to happen here unless I get some lotion for my hands," Mary says.

A female guard leads Mary, Regina and Michelle into the room. The guard sees the distress on Mary's face from not having her lotion. Before leaving the room, the guard tells Mary she will try to find some lotion for her

Tim continues walking down the hall toward another area. Tim has the role of connecting with other security staff to bring Oshea to the meeting.

A guard approaches the dining room table where Oshea is sitting. The guard tells Oshea it's time for him to head to a waiting room to meet up with Tim.

Oshea looks up at the guard. "I'm ready."

As he prepares to leave, an inmate who knows what Oshea is about to do walks up to him. He and Oshea have talked for several weeks about his meeting with Mary. "Hey man, it'll be okay," the inmate tells him. "You doin' the right thing. I wish I could do what you're about to do."

Oshea and the inmate shake hands and give each other a quick shoulder bump.

The inmate watches Oshea exit the dining area. A tear trickles down the inmate's face – happiness for Oshea and regret for himself that he doesn't have the same opportunity.

Oshea is led to a waiting room where Tim is there to greet him. Tim wants to go over final details of the meeting before he escorts him to see Mary. The meeting is scheduled for 90 minutes.

The female guard is smiling when she enters the meeting room. She has a small tube of lotion for Mary's hands.

Mary lets out a deep sigh of relief and says, "Thank you Jesus!" She rubs the lotion on her hands so fast that she pays no attention to the brand name of the lotion. Mary passes the lotion to Michelle, who then gives it to Regina.

Mary and Regina are sitting next to each other at the conference table. When Regina finishes with the lotion, she glances at the tube and stares at it. Regina looks up at the ceiling shaking her head.

Mary sees Regina's reaction. "What's the matter?" she asks.

"Girl, you need to look at the name of this lotion."

"What do you mean?"

Regina gives the tube to Mary. "Look at that!"

Mary's eyes get wide when she sees the name of the lotion.

"Beyond Belief! Oh, my God!"

Regina and Mary look at each other and have the same thoughts. They understand that what's about to happen is truly beyond belief. Mary and Regina don't have much time to discuss the irony of the lotion's name.

Tim and Oshea have left the waiting room and are heading down the hall to the meeting room. As they get closer to the room, Regina can hear footsteps. Mary hears the same sound. Both stare at the door.

Sherlinda, who played a key role in getting this meeting confirmed, is standing outside the meeting room waiting on Tim and Oshea, particularly Oshea. Sherlinda is among a contingent of Stillwater staff who came to work on their off day as a show of support for the meeting. "You better be good in there," Sherlinda tells him in a playful stern voice, trying to hide her smile.

Oshea nods his head. "I will." He goes through the door.

Tim follows.

A silent tension immediately grips the room when Oshea enters.

Nervous anticipation is visible on the faces of all five people – Mary, Regina, Tim, Michelle and Oshea.

Is this going to work? Will 12 years of anger erupt from inside of Mary? Will it make her leap out of her chair and yell at Oshea, *"WHY DID YOU KILL MY SON?"*

That's the last thing Tim, Michelle and the rest of the DOC want to see. Tim has seen Victim Offender Dialogues at other correctional facilities in Minnesota not end well. If Mary and Oshea don't have a positive outcome, it would be a setback for the DOC's attempts to develop a restorative justice program at Stillwater.

Mary remains seated at the wooden conference table, but the flashbacks taunt her again, almost as if they are teasing her, testing her at this crucial moment to see if she is truly serious about her search for forgiveness. Her eyes are fixated on Oshea as he walks toward the table.

His head is down, looking at nothing in particular on the floor.

An image instantly pops up in Mary's mind, projecting painful memories she has not forgotten. She sees a younger Oshea aiming a gun at Laramiun in that living room and firing those four shots into his body. As Laramiun falls to the floor, Mary hears him call out to her: "Momma!!!" The cry of Laramiun's voice sends a slight jolt through Mary's body while she sits at the table.

Another flashback surfaces. Mary is jabbed with the image of her horrifying scream at work when she learns Laramiun is dead. Nobody in the room is aware of the internal torment that Mary is dealing with when she sees Oshea for the first time since the last day of the trial 12 years ago.

Oshea doesn't make eye contact with Mary until he reaches the table. He breaks the tension in the room when he leans over the table to extend his hand.

Mary, still seated, extends her hand for a soft but quick handshake. She is sitting directly across the table from Oshea.

Tim and Michelle are seated in chairs a few feet away.

Oshea can barely settle into his seat before Mary starts the conversation, looking intently at Oshea, "I don't know you and you don't know me, and you didn't know my son," Mary says to Oshea. "We need to come to some type of understanding."

"Yes Ma'am," Oshea replies.

Months of preparation for this meeting by Tim, Michelle and other DOC staff suddenly goes out the window. Tim was supposed to lay out ground rules for the conversation when Oshea arrived in the room, but Mary takes it upon herself to call the meeting to order.

Tim and Michelle look at each other with mild surprise. Because of their longtime friendship, words are not necessary – nor an interruption. They can tell this is one of those moments when you just go with the flow.

Apparently, the strength that Mary asked God to give her in the lobby bathroom has kicked in. She sits up in her chair, leans forward slightly and displays an air of confidence. She proceeds to tell Oshea about Laramiun and his childhood, how he liked to go fishing with family members and his dreams of having a boat someday.

Since Mary was not allowed to bring pictures of Laramiun into the room, she gives Oshea a visual of her son as much as she can. Mary continues talking about Laramiun for several minutes, prompting an interjection from Oshea.

"Sounds like he and I could have been friends."

"Maybe," Mary replies.

The mood softens even more when Mary tells Oshea that Laramiun didn't like school much and didn't finish high school.

"That was me too," Oshea said smiling. "My mother always got on me about how I was in school. I used to think school was boring."

Mary and Oshea share a quick, but subdued laugh. Both have not forgotten the real reason why they are in this room, yet Mary persists with a family-style approach to the conversation. She asks Oshea about his early childhood.

Oshea tells Mary about his mother and her job as a truck driver in Illinois when he was little. He recalls going on trips with her when she had to leave town for several days. Oshea smiles when he talks about growing up in Kankakee and spending part of the summers with his family on Chicago's South Side.

"So, when did you move to Minnesota?" Mary asks.

"1988. I was 12. My mom had friends in Minneapolis who were trying to get us to move there. She finally decided to do it. I was okay with it."

Tim and Michelle look at each other again.

Regina had already made occasional glances at Tim and Michelle during the conversation, wondering if either one of them has intentions of getting involved in this get-acquainted session.

Tim and Michelle remain quiet.

For nearly an hour, Mary and Oshea are having what amounts to a casual discussion about their families and interests. Throughout Mary's extensive preparation process to have this meeting with Oshea, she was adamant with Tim and Michelle about her mission. Three items in particular were always at the top of her list:

- Find out why he changed his name.
- What happened at the party and why.
- Can she really forgive him?

Mary hasn't come close to addressing any one of these three objectives, and there's only about 30 minutes left to get it done. Tim, Michelle and Regina have been glued to every word spoken by Mary and Oshea. The tone of the conversation is the most surprising element for Tim, who has a pretty good feel on how these dialogues can turn out. From coordinating these sessions at other facilities, Tim can sense within a few minutes if a dialogue will be productive or come to a premature end. With Mary and Oshea, Tim isn't sure.

One thing is certain, Mary is relaxed and dictating the direction of this meeting. She has made a remarkable shift from the woman who was in tears entering the prison. The woman stressing about not having any lotion for her hands and battling anxieties in the prison lobby is not the woman who has been sitting across the table from a convicted murderer for the past hour.

This woman is in control. In Mary's mind, she has already won a major battle. She has fought off demons of hate, fear and uncertainty to get to this point, to come face-to-face with the man who took her son's life. Mary is in a moment of empowerment! No regulations or objectives will stop her from getting vindication – or forgiveness – the way she wants it!

As time ticks away in the final half hour, Michelle is compelled to break her silence. She knows what Mary wants to find out in the meeting and tries to steer her in that direction.

"Mary, we know you had some questions you wanted to get to," Michelle says.

"I know." Mary essentially dismisses Michelle's reminder and gives a subtle message to everyone in the room that she's still in charge. She turns her attention back to Oshea. "So, what kind of training or activities are you doing here?"

"It seems like a long time ago, but I got my GED in '95. I made a promise to my mom to finish high school. Since then, I learned how to cook a little bit. I've got a baking certificate, been taking some classes and doing a lot of reading. I started a reading group for some of the guys in here. We read books and talk about what we read."

Mary nods her head. "That's nice."

The preparation process that Mary went through is really starting to pay off now. As Oshea continues to talk about his activities in prison, she's beginning to see him more as a human being – not the animal she had called him.

For years, Mary wondered how ruthless Oshea could have been as a 16-year-old kid to shoot down her son in a house party with other people nearby in the living room. Suppose Oshea had shot wildly in the heat of the moment, hitting Laramiun as well as another person. Mary often thought about Oshea's lack of concern for the lives of others when he fired at Laramiun.

For years, Mary also had questionable thoughts about Oshea's mother. How could a mother take her 16-year-old son to an adult after-hours party?

With only a few minutes remaining for the meeting, Mary has yet to ask about the shooting at the party or why Oshea's mother took him along. Or why he changed his name. Throughout the preparation process, Oshea was told he would have to address those issues when Mary asked him face-to-face. Oshea told Tim in the preparation meetings that he was willing to be honest and sincere with Mary about those topics, a key factor in the meeting getting confirmed. If Oshea was unwilling to go down that road with Mary, the meeting would not have happened.

Oshea seems ready to talk about the shooting, but Mary seems to have developed another strategy. Whatever the plan is, Mary has been piecing it together while talking with Oshea.

Tim looks at his watch. He knows the time is approaching to wrap up this social hour and escort Oshea back to his cell block. Tim looks at Michelle – then glances at Regina. All three have a look of bewilderment on their faces.

As Mary and Oshea continue chatting, Tim accepts the surprising realization that Mary is not going to have the opportunity to meet her three objectives. Even if Mary interrupts Oshea while he's talking about his prison activities, there wouldn't be enough time to get into the three topics.

The ultimate goal of Victim Offender Dialogues is to have the victim and offender discuss the crime and reach some sort of reconciliation or understanding. It is very apparent to Tim, Michelle and Regina that this is not going to happen today.

Just when Tim is about to tell Mary and Oshea the meeting must come to an end, Mary makes a stunning comment.

"Would you be interested in meeting again?"

The question leads Tim to believe that maybe Mary wants to meet again with Oshea to get her answers on the party and his name change – and whether or not she has forgiven him. But there's a problem. The DOC frowns on follow-up meetings in VOD's. The sessions are intended to be one-time gatherings. There are no sequels while an offender is incarcerated. Tim and Michelle, baffled by Mary's question, want to respond but Oshea answers first without hesitation, "Yeah, I wouldn't mind that."

Tim fumbles for an answer. "We'll have to let you know if we can do that…That's something we'll have to talk about among the staff here."

"Okay. Let me know," Mary says.

"Well, everybody, on that note, we need to bring this meeting to a close," Tim says. "Mary and

Regina, thank you for coming. Oshea. Thank you for your participation and your cooperation."

Oshea is looking at Mary and gives her some reassurance on her question. "If they work it out for us to talk again, I'll make myself available," Oshea says with a slight grin.

Mary nods her head in agreement. "Thank you."

Oshea, still looking at Mary, offers one more comment before getting up from his chair. His grin disappears. "I want you to know that I would never do anything to hurt you again."

Oshea's words freeze Mary as she looks back at him. She's silent with no expression on her face, but her eyes are fluttering as if they're trying to speak for her. Mary struggles to comprehend what she just heard. The man who took her son's life expressed remorse to her, words she thought for years she would never hear.

Mary is still speechless as Tim, Michelle and Regina get up from their chairs. Mary and Oshea also get up from their chairs.

Mary turns to Regina, her rock of support throughout this process. Mary is hoping Regina gives her an answer on what to say or what to do next.

Oshea makes a request to help Mary break her silence, "Ma'am. Before I go, may I give you a hug?"

Mary's head tilts slightly in amazement. This is the last thing she expected as part of her mission. The man who killed her son wants to give her a hug. Her first thoughts were. *How crazy is this? This really is beyond belief!* But Oshea's question touches a nerve with Mary. It breaks Mary's silence and generates a nervous smile. "Okay."

Mary's nervousness is shared by Tim and Michelle. Tim immediately thinks about VOD regulations, which prohibit inmates from initiating physical contact. Oshea already broke that rule when he reached over the table to shake Mary's hand at the beginning of the meeting. Nothing was said about that encounter and Tim is unsure of stepping in to head off this one.

If Tim is thinking of saying no to the hug, he's too late. Mary is slowly making her way around the table toward Oshea. Her eyes are tearing and her body is trembling.

Tim and Michelle can see what's about to happen. Both know a hug is against VOD protocol, but there seems to be something safe and appropriate with this moment and neither want to spoil it. No guards have been in the room for the entire meeting and none are present at the conclusion. Tim and Michelle are in charge, and they are making an executive decision to let this hug happen.

Oshea opens his arms, as Mary gets closer to him.

Tim is standing behind Oshea. As soon as Mary and Oshea embrace, Mary's legs give way and she begins to collapse. A symphony of heartache, emotions and submission overwhelm her. Oshea has to tighten his hold on Mary to keep her from falling to the floor. Mary is in the strong arms of the man who took her son's life, a man now trying to comfort her.

Mary's head lands on his shoulder. She cries uncontrollably while Oshea holds her up.

Tim doesn't move. He remains standing behind Oshea.

Michelle and Regina are motionless at the table. The three of them appear to be frozen by the drama of this totally unexpected event.

A tear trickles down Regina's face. She understands what this moment means for her friend.

Mary's sobbing gets louder, but she still hasn't said anything while Oshea holds onto her.

His hands gently rub Mary's shoulder and her upper back. "I got you," Oshea whispers softly to Mary.

Mary came to Stillwater Correctional Facility wondering if she could express forgiveness. But in this moment, she's making an even greater discovery. A bond has been birthed. Oshea has had few opportunities to hug his mother over the past 12 years. Mary can't remember the last time she hugged Laramiun before his death. Both appear to be comforting each other for the absence of a loved one in their lives.

For Mary and Oshea, this hug is far more than an emotional embrace. It's a symbolic culmination for two individuals who have come full circle with their feelings and actions.

Twelve years ago, Oshea had a different name. He was a defiant, troublesome teenager with no trace of compassion for killing a man he didn't know.

Mary was an angry woman who believed her son didn't deserve to die like that. Not only was she mad at the convicted assailant, she often questioned God, her Lord and Savior, for allowing it to happen. Now, Mary could feel the grace of God that led her into Oshea's arms, telling her that the time has come to let go completely and forgive.

The beginning of total forgiveness ignites with their embrace, yet Oshea has to be a willing and supportive participant. Oshea buys into this time-frozen episode and continues to hold onto Mary, reaching his own pinnacle of forgiveness for what he did at that house party. The hug has surpassed a minute, but it seems much longer. Two lives are changing in this embrace.

As much as Tim and Michelle are marveling at this tender connection, Tim has to end it. He needs to get Oshea back to his cell block. Tim edges forward to touch Oshea and Mary to let them know they have to separate.

As Oshea lets Mary go, he asks, "You okay?"

Mary doesn't say anything. Her face is wet from tears. She brings both hands to her face. Her eyes are closed. She doesn't see Tim leading Oshea out of the room.

Oshea looks back at her one more time.

Mary's body flinches when Tim closes the door behind him.

Inside the meeting room is a bathroom, but Mary continues to stand in the spot where she and Oshea hugged. If Mary is planning to talk to God about what just happened, the conversation is going to take place right here near the table. Mary is giving no indication of wanting to move or sit down.

Regina walks over to Mary to comfort her. Before Regina gets to her, Mary extends her arms outward with the palms of her hands facing up. She bends over slightly as if she's in pain. But she's not. Her legs are strong now. When Regina touches Mary's arm, Mary suddenly has the strength to speak. "I just hugged the man who murdered my son," Mary said softly, her voice cracking.

Mary, still bent over, repeats herself. This time her voice is a little louder.

*"I just hugged the man who murdered my son!"*

Regina is holding Mary's arm as Mary slowly rises up from her bent position. Mary takes a deep breath, raises her voice another level and exhales.

*"I just hugged the man who murdered my son! I think I have really forgiven this man! Oh, my God!"*

Mary is standing straight. Her arms are elevated, palms up. Her head is tilted up. Eyes now open. If the ceiling wasn't blocking Mary's view, she would be looking straight into heaven, perhaps telling Laramiun, *"Son, I'm okay...I'm at peace now."*

This prison conference room has been transformed into a church service. As if she's in church on a Sunday morning, Mary is out of her seat embracing the powerful words of her pastor's sermon and the spirit of her Heavenly Father. The only thing missing is the timely cadence of an organ. She bounces on her feet a few times, almost allowing the Holy Spirit to ease her into a happy dance.

More tears flow down her face, but they are tears of joy this time. She has finally found peace in her injured soul – and forgiveness. Mary can feel the demons of hatred, bitterness and anger escaping from her body. Her spirit is reborn. In a matter of minutes, emphatic minutes, the burden and pain she has felt all these years is lifted.

Deliverance made its way into this conference room.

Mary is experiencing a freedom she has never felt before. This meeting, capped by an unpredictable, unforgettable hug, has set her free! She now has a true understanding of forgiveness. Teaching 'forgiveness' in the Sunday school class at her church was not enough. The class was the springboard, but Mary needed to experience the full measure of forgiveness to be whole as a Christian and move forward with her mission of helping mothers like herself.

It all made sense now for Mary. She could read Colossians 3:13 in the Bible and honestly identify with it. And feel it.

*"Bearing with one another, and if one has a complaint against another, forgiving each other. As the Lord has forgiven you, so you also must forgive." (ESV)*

Mary didn't get the opportunity to tell Oshea that she had forgiven him before he left the room. The hug was all the communication they needed. Forgiveness has been finalized for both of them.

Regina gives Mary a moment to regroup and acknowledge Her Lord and Savior in this long-awaited moment. Mary is praying softly as Regina, her eyes streaming with tears, admires what her friend has done. She grabs Mary's hands. "I'm so proud of you…You did it, girl! You did it!"

Mary isn't sure what she did. "Girl, I don't know how or what just happened in here. This ain't nothing but God's work. Thank you Jesus! That's all I can say. Thank you Jesus!"

Tim is sitting with Oshea in a holding room down the hall. He has to wait with Oshea until a guard comes to escort him back to his cell block. Tim is giving Oshea a few minutes to digest what he just went through. Tim wants to ask Oshea the obvious how-was-it question, but he holds off.

Oshea is in a pensive mood. He's far less talkative than he was during his conversation with Mary.

He eventually interrupts Tim's thoughts, "Is she going to be okay?" Oshea asks Tim.

"I'll check on her when I go back down there. Regina and Michelle are with her."

When Oshea left the room, Mary was in tears holding her hands to her face. Because of the dramatic ending, Tim reminds Oshea that the VOD program provides access to a counselor if he wants to talk about the meeting.

A guard enters the room to take Oshea to his cell block. Before Oshea leaves, Tim extends his hand and offers a reassuring comment.

"You did great in there, Oshea."

"Thanks." As Oshea walks toward his cell block, he's unaware that his monumental meeting with Mary is the beginning of a remarkable journey.

Tim hurriedly walks back to the conference room to check on Mary. When he gets there, the atmosphere is completely different.

The room is cheerful, a complete turnaround from the tension and anxiety that filled the room when everyone first walked in almost two hours ago. Mary, Regina and Michelle are standing together smiling and chatting. Relief and fulfillment are on the faces of all three women.

The sight of Mary smiling puts a grin on Tim's face as he walks over to give her a hug. "I'm so happy for you," he tells Mary. "What a wonderful moment for you. You did great."

Though Mary didn't verbally express her forgiveness to Oshea, or resolve two of her three objectives – what really happened at the party and why did he change his name – the first Victim Offender Dialogue at Stillwater Correctional

Facility is considered a major success. The outcome gives the Minnesota DOC the momentum it was looking for to move forward with plans to expand its restorative justice program at Stillwater.

Mary is still smiling as she prepares to leave the conference room with Tim, Michelle and Regina to head toward the security entrance.

In Mary's hand is the tube of "Beyond Belief" lotion that helped calm her nerves when she walked into the room.

Who would have imagined that a tube of lotion would end up having more value than softening a person's skin? The tube became a lasting souvenir for Mary. She is not about to leave that tube on the table. The connection is too powerful for Mary to leave it behind.

Mary is upbeat when she goes through the security checkpoint. The guard that checked in the group is staring at Mary, wondering if this is the same woman who was so agitated when she passed through his station.

The guard is right. This is not the same woman.

Mary is not the fragile, fearful woman who was unsure if she could stand up to her spiritual challenge. Mary is walking out of Stillwater as a conqueror. The glow on her face confirms her victory.

Tim takes several group pictures of Mary, Regina and Michelle in the lobby – another souvenir for Mary to cherish on this memorable day. At the moment, only the five people in that room know what transpired in the meeting.

The privacy of that meeting wouldn't last long.

Mary and Oshea Israel after his release from prison.

**FORGIVING YOU IS MY GIFT TO YOU. MOVING ON IS MY GIFT TO MYSELF.**

# CHAPTER TEN

### *Mary and Oshea become 'family'*
*March 27, 2005*

Mary is having a joyful Sunday morning in church, still glowing from the aftermath of her life-changing meeting with Oshea the day before. Her hand clapping is emphatic while she stands and bounces to the beat of an energetic song performed by the choir.

Mary called her pastor yesterday when she returned home from Stillwater to share the news of her glorious experience. The pastor set aside some time in today's service for Mary to tell the congregation about her deliverance. The invitation to testify is the beginning of a much more enjoyable journey for Mary.

As Mary talks to the congregation about her meeting with Oshea, she doesn't realize the enormity of the groundwork she's laying after her experience. All of the community outreach Mary did while working for US West would pale in comparison to what's ahead. Testimonies will soon have a much larger audience for Mary and Oshea.

Mary's church members are the first to hear her story. Her message is powerful and thought-provoking. She speaks for about 20 minutes, drawing several bursts of "Amen" and "Praise God!" from the congregation. Some members shake their head in amazement while listening to Mary. For many of them, it's beyond belief that they would be able to do what Mary has done – forgive a person who has taken the life of a loved one.

How could Mary bring herself to a place in her soul and spirit where she forgives the man who murdered her son? How could she do that? The questions are visible on the faces of church members, but Mary is providing the answers, and she's doing it with passion and confidence.

Mary's words are strong, yet comforting. She stresses the importance of forgiveness and how it leads to fulfillment in the eyes of God. Mary's public speaking days with US West has made a quick return. Victory is evident in her eyes and vocal tone as she recaps how she made the commitment to find forgiveness.

The congregation is looking at a changed woman, and Mary knows it. She proclaims her spirit has been re-born, that her life has been blessed with a new purpose. Mary receives a standing ovation when she concludes her speech.

A smile comes across her face, but she knows she hasn't done all of this alone. She looks up, extends her arms outward and says softly, "Thank you Jesus! Thank you Jesus!"

*March 28, 2005*

Two days after his meeting with Mary, Oshea is back to his kitchen duties serving meals to fellow inmates.

Sherlinda is walking briskly down the hall toward the kitchen carrying a notebook with folders containing documents. One of the documents has Oshea's name on it. Sherlinda enters the kitchen area and heads straight for Oshea. "I heard you did really well in your meeting with Mary," Sherlinda states with a grin.

"Yeah, thanks. It got a little deep at the end, but it was cool."

"I heard." Sherlinda nods.

"You heard about the hug?"

"Yep! You know that was against the rules."

"Maybe it was, but it was about the moment. It seemed like the right thing to do."

"No big deal. We're all very proud of you. I have something for you." Sherlinda hands Oshea the sheet of paper with his name on it.

It's a letter confirming his selection to Stillwater's new restorative justice committee. She's in charge of the committee and is convinced Oshea will be a valuable asset in Stillwater's efforts to develop a restorative justice program.

Oshea is among several Stillwater inmates invited to be on the committee. Sherlinda asks Oshea to help teach a class appropriately titled, "Restorative Justice 101." Oshea's "teaching" background makes him a good fit for the assignment because of his work with the book club he started. He also completed a course in prison on "Families And Focus."

If Stillwater is looking for a face for its restorative justice program, Oshea appears to be the leading candidate. A key requirement for inmates to remain on the committee is writing an apology letter to the victim. The letters are not sent to the victims, but writing the letter is their way of participating in a VOD and measuring their sincerity.

Oshea's letter to Mary is easy to write. He has an insightful and emotional meeting to use as a resource.

Mary's testimony at her church generates a buzz around Minneapolis. Church members begin to spread the story, leading to speaking invitations for Mary at other churches and various organizations.

With a clear conscience and spirit, Mary is motivated to move forward in establishing her own organization to help mothers who have endured similar pain of losing a child to violence.

In June of 2005, Michelle, Regina and Tim join Mary and a few other close associates at a Minneapolis restaurant to have the first meeting as an organization under the name **"From Death To Life."**

When Regina suggested the name for the organization more than a year ago, Mary wasn't ready to make her cause more public. She's ready now.

The meeting is a breakthrough for Mary's vision and becomes the catalyst for her story to be heard around the country.

A month later, Tim and Michelle arrange for Mary and Oshea to meet again at Stillwater. The meeting is far less dramatic this time and more enlightening about the future.

As with the first meeting, Mary does not ask Oshea about the party or why he changed his name. Mary tells Michelle and Tim that, "It isn't important to her anymore."

Mary did achieve one of her three objectives in the first meeting with her forgiveness of Oshea. For Mary, that was her main accomplishment.

The second meeting, however, establishes an important protocol: Mary and Oshea agree to work together to tell their story, even while Oshea remains in prison. Upon his release, they agree to continue their association and let people know that forgiveness is possible – no matter how painful the hurt.

The first collaboration between Mary and Oshea comes on Nov. 17, 2005 at Stillwater.

Sherlinda's restorative justice committee wants to do an event to help promote the committee's work. An appearance by Mary and Oshea was requested and later approved by Stillwater officials.

***In front of about 150 inmates, Mary and Oshea make a symbolic appearance, which begins with Mary introducing Oshea as her "Spiritual Son."***

Think about this for a moment! Mary is calling Oshea her "Spiritual Son." The word *son* alone is worth a pause in thought. Mary has embraced forgiveness to the point of welcoming Oshea into her world as her "Spiritual Son." It's an affectionate label for Oshea, who met Mary on her terms when both were seeking reconciliation.

Oshea would never replace Laramiun, and Mary will never forget him, but Mary is perfectly content with giving Oshea an almost unbelievable status in her life after the crime he committed.

In this context, forgiveness is truly a powerful thing!

Could you do what Mary has done?

Could you forgive the person that took a loved one's life and become "spiritual friends" with them? Or go as far as Mary did and welcome the person as a "spiritual family" member? This topic will obviously generate long debates. Understandably, some people who suffered the loss of a loved one to violence will have an immediate answer, ***"Hell no!"***

During Mary and Oshea's presentation at Stillwater, several inmates in the audience stood up to tell Mary they knew Laramiun and expressed their condolences to her.

Near the end of Oshea's speech, the event takes a heartbreaking turn. An inmate stands up to tell Oshea he wishes he could be in his shoes, wishing he had the opportunity to express remorse to his victim. Tears stream down the inmate's face.

Two more inmates stand up to offer similar feelings of regret. Nearly everyone in the room is trying to fight back tears – caught up in the emotional and humanistic conclusion of Mary and Oshea's story.

Oshea now understands how fortunate he is to be able to experience redemption.

The heartfelt reaction from inmates is vindication for the DOC to continue pushing for a restorative justice program at Stillwater.

Word spreads throughout the DOC system about Mary and Oshea's appearance. Other correctional facilities in Minnesota submit requests to have them speak to their inmates.

The Stillwater appearance is further evidence of a stronger bond developing between Mary and Oshea, and that bond is going to take them places they never imagined.

Oshea gets permission to join Mary for outside appearances while he's incarcerated, but nothing changes about his sentence. He still must serve at least 17 years for his second-degree murder conviction.

Two years after Mary and Oshea's Stillwater presentation, the DOC and the University of Minnesota team up on a research project to study the effects of Victim Offender Dialogues. Eighteen offenders at various Minnesota prisons between 1993 and 2007 are included in the study.

Before participating in a VOD, the 18 offenders had a combined 184 violations, including 115 major violations.

After a dialogue, the group had a total of seven violations. The results prove that VODs can have a positive impact on offender behavior. Oshea had no more violations after meeting with Mary, although his transformation was apparent before the meeting. Several of the 18 offenders in the study expressed a common theme: the VOD is a "life-changing" experience.

*March 10, 2007*

Mary's From Death To Life organization is more visible and active. The organization has become an outlet for mothers like herself, as well as a platform to stand up against crime and violence, particularly in North Minneapolis.

Mary grew up in North Minneapolis and has chosen to remain in the community. Every second Saturday of the month, she and members of her organization march to the parking lot of a major grocery store chain on West Broadway to raise awareness of crime and the plight of mothers who have lost children to violence. The grieving mothers regularly walk with Mary.

Whenever there's a fatal shooting, particularly of a young person, Mary rounds up her members to hold prayer vigils at the scene or visit the victim's family. The activities of From Death To Life lead to more speaking engagements for her to tell her story, as well as the story of mothers in her organization.

On this day, Mary is speaking at an event called Women of Great Hope and Vision at St. Phillips Catholic Church. A group of nuns from the Visitation Monastery in Minneapolis are in the audience, along with a man named Brian Mogren, who runs St. Jane House, a hospitality center in North Minneapolis.

Mogren and the Visitation Sisters collaborate on projects and events to help struggling residents in North Minneapolis. They live in the community, so they are fully aware of the disparities and poverty gripping large sections of the area. But they don't know Mary. They have only heard about Mary's work and her organization. The unfamiliarity is about to change.

Mogren and the Visitation Sisters are so moved by Mary's story that they all approach her after the presentation to introduce themselves.

Sister Mary Margaret McKenzie is the first to say hello and praise Mary for her story, followed by Sister Mary Frances Reis, Sister Suzanne Homeyer and Mogren.

The conversation leads to an invitation for Mary to speak next weekend at the Visitation Sisters' community meeting. Another bond is born. The Visitation Sisters tell Mary they would like to support her organization and provide resources. For the Visitation Sisters, Mary's mission gives them an additional platform to support North Minneapolis.

Mogren also makes a key gesture. The Visitation Sisters have occasional events at St. Jane House, a three-story home that can accommodate residents and meetings. Mogren's interest in Mary's mission prompts him to offer St. Jane House as a permanent home for her Saturday meetings. The offer brings more stability to Mary's organization.

Since starting From Death To Life, Mary has had to move her meetings to different locations. Mary returns the kindness by inviting Mogren and Sister Mary Margaret to join her board of directors.

Sister Mary Margaret extends her involvement a little further by attending the regular Saturday sessions and becoming a "spiritual advisor" for Mary in the meetings and beyond. Mary often confides in Sister Mary Margaret about things in her life and what she's been through, creating sort of a mother-daughter relationship.

The more Mary talks about Oshea, the more Sister Mary Margaret is intrigued by him. She tells Mary that she hopes to meet him someday. Since Sister Mary Margaret likes to think of Mary as a "daughter," that would make Oshea Sister Mary Margaret's …?

Mary has built a component within From Death To Life called "Two Mothers," the theme of her Saturday morning healing sessions where mothers of children lost to violence come together. Among the mothers who sought out Mary for healing is Regina Anne Smith, a mother of five boys when she moved to Minneapolis in 1991. She now has four. Her 16 year-old son, Maurice, was fatally shot in 1997 in an accidental shooting. Maurice was riding his bicycle in North Minneapolis when a gunman struck him while aiming at someone else. The assailant received a life sentence, but that was no consolation for Smith. Her son died because of a beef between two people he didn't know.

"It's hard to put into words what Mary's activities have done for me," Smith says. "You lose a child and you don't know how to go on. You get a chance to talk at the meetings and share your pain but you know you're not alone, and that's the main thing."

On the final Saturday of each month, Mary makes the challenging attempt to bring together mothers from both sides of a crime – the mothers of a victim and mothers of the offenders. Mary fully understands the importance of dialogue between two mothers affected by the same crime. Healing can only come when you sit at the table together. Mary has lived it, which gives her the motivation to help bring peace and understanding for women on both sides of tragedy.

*March 1, 2010*

Oshea Israel, formerly known as Marlon Rockshawn Green, walks out of Red Wing (Minn.) Correctional Facility into a van that will take him to a halfway house in Minneapolis. Before he gets into the van, he turns around looks at the facility. It's a somber, yet comforting feeling for Oshea to know that he's no longer incarcerated.

Oshea is on probation until August 2018, but at least he's free from the walls, bars and isolated cells.

Nine days later, Oshea is treated to a welcome home celebration at St. Jane's House. About 30 people attend the festive occasion, including Mary, the Visitation Sisters, members of Mary's board of directors and several community leaders.

The celebration stops momentarily to gather everybody in a circle to express support and well wishes to Oshea. When it's time for Sister Mary Margaret to take her turn, the circle gets quiet. People in the circle know how close she is to Mary and how she has been by her side through difficult times.

Regardless of Mary's relationship with Oshea, Laramiun will always be her first-born child, and occasionally, Sister Mary Margaret has had to wipe away Mary's tears.

While being there for Mary, Sister Mary Margaret was embracing Oshea from a distance. Today, she gets to see her prayers answered face-to-face. A tear comes down Sister Mary Margaret's face as she begins her testimony.

Other tears in the circle begin to flow.

"You've been so dear to me…like a grandson," she says to Oshea. "I could be your Grandma!"

Now we know the "official connection" between Oshea and Sister Mary Margaret. Several people in the circle, including Mary, wipe away tears in this joyous moment. Everybody in the room is touched by the aura of forgiveness. This circle was generated by a loss of life, but forgiveness is allowing people to move on with their lives without the burden of guilt, hatred, anger or bitterness.

After Sister Mary Margaret's emotional tribute to Oshea, the circle erupts into hugs, smiles and harmony. There is peace and love in this room.

Mary and Oshea helped create the atmosphere behind prison walls.

*March 21, 2010*

Now that Oshea has limited freedom – he still has to report back to the halfway house by nightfall each day – he and Mary take the first step toward their next journey.

The Basilica of St. Mary's Church in downtown Minneapolis invited Mary and Oshea to speak at an event. It's the first public appearance for Mary and Oshea since his release from prison.

Word spreads again on this compelling story in the coming months, leading to more speaking engagements around Minnesota and nearby states. But the story takes off nationally a year later when CBS Evening News airs a short piece on Mary and Oshea.

A month after the CBS Evening News story, Oshea is on an airplane for the first time in his life. He and Mary are heading to northern California, all expenses paid, to speak at Menlo Park Presbyterian Church. Menlo Park pastor John Ortberg saw the

CBS Evening News story and quickly made arrangements for Mary and Oshea to travel to his church.

While on the plane, it finally sinks in for Mary that this thing called forgiveness is real. She and Oshea are sitting together, but she doesn't get a chance to share her revelation with Oshea. Oshea has dozed off. Mary glances at him and says to herself, shaking her head slightly, "Wow, this really is beyond belief…I'm traveling with the man who took my son from me…"

More media coverage follows for Mary and Oshea, including a short story in People Magazine in September of 2011. Four days later, Mary and Oshea are in New York appearing on the popular TV show The View. Mary and Oshea end up taking three trips to Washington, D.C., between 2011 and 2012 – two of the trips related to the Conference of Fair Sentencing for Youth. Oshea's case was used as an example in the fight against life sentences without parole for juveniles. Mary and Oshea spoke on a panel at the 2012 convention and were presented an award in 2011.

Mary made two international trips without Oshea – to Assissi, Italy for the Conference On Love And Forgiveness in September 2012 and to Amman, Jordan in February 2014 for a conference sponsored by the Fetzer Institute. During the trip, she met the Prince of Jordan. Accompanying Mary on the trip to Jordan was Ed Roy, a man she had met at one of her speaking engagements in 2006. Ed introduced himself to Mary after her speech and talked about how he was feeling similar pain after the shooting death of his son a few months earlier. Another bonding moment for Mary.

Mary and Ed kept in touch over the years. Ed began to attend speaking engagements with Mary and later joined her From Death To Life board. Ed is now Mary's husband. The couple married on Jan. 3, 2015 and Mary's "Spiritual Son" was in the wedding. During the reception, Mary and Oshea danced together for the "mother-son" ritual.

There are times when life really can be beyond belief…

Mary and Oshea at an outdoor speaking engagement in Minneapolis.

Mary and Oshea on one of their two trips to
Washington, D.C.

# CHAPTER ELEVEN

### A mother's eternal agony
*'I hurt every day because of a bad decision'*

On the night of Feb. 11, 1993, Carolyn Green, a dedicated and caring mother, asked her 16 year old son if he wanted to go with her to an after-hours house party. Carolyn was going with a few of her friends and wasn't intending to stay long because she was leaving town early the next morning.

The question to her son, and her son agreeing to go with her, changed both of their lives forever.

For Carolyn, that fateful night in Minneapolis continues to haunt her.

"I'm not at peace," she says in a conversation in early March 2017. "I hurt every day because of a bad decision. I know I had a role in what happened that night. I feel the mistake I made. I've been badly broken…into a lot of tiny pieces."

There's a reason why Mary Johnson-Roy incorporates the "Two Mothers" program into her From Death To Life organization. In many homicide cases, two mothers experience the pain of tragedy – the mother of the victim and the mother of the offender.

Carolyn's pain was even more agonizing when she had to watch her son, Marlon, being led away to prison for a 25-year sentence. Marlon, today known as Oshea Israel, was convicted of second-degree murder for fatally shooting Mary's son, Laramiun Byrd, at the house party.

Carolyn didn't pull the trigger, but she can't escape the guilty feelings. It's been that way for her since that night. "I pray about it every day; I think about it every day," says Carolyn, who no longer lives in Minnesota. "I have shed more tears than I can count. Did I love my child too much? Is that what happened? Can you love somebody too much? Is that the question I can't answer? You can't blame yourself, but I do. I thought I was protecting my son by keeping him with me."

Oshea, present during the conversation, steps in to console his mother and deflect the blame. "Things happen Momma," Oshea says. "That was my decision to do what I did. If it didn't happen that night, I would have killed somebody else another time. I was out there in those streets."

Oshea's comments give Carolyn a slight measure of peace but not much. She had to live without her son for 17 years. The prison term might have been longer if Oshea, now 43, had been an adult.

"If my son hadn't got locked up, maybe I wouldn't have him today," Carolyn says. "Everything happens for a reason. We can't always put our hand on the reason why. You have to accept that."

Carolyn, now 63, has had to "share" Oshea with Mary, who calls him her "Spiritual Son" after their first meeting in prison. Mary continues to refer to Oshea as her "Spiritual Son" during speaking engagements. Carolyn says she's okay with the relationship Mary has built with her son and how she has forgiven him for what he did.

"It's an amazing thing, a blessing," Carolyn says of Mary. "I can appreciate it. She's proven her forgiveness."

Will Carolyn be able to forgive herself some day?

# The birth of 'Beyond Belief'

This true, remarkable story was born out of the love and compassion a group of nuns in North Minneapolis showed, and continue to show today, for Mary Johnson-Roy.

The nuns are known as the Visitation Sisters, although many residents in the predominantly African-American community refer to them as "Sisters In The Hood" because of their kind-hearted gestures and dedicated service to people in need. The primary Visitation Sisters include:

* Sister Mary Margaret McKenzie
* Sister Mary Frances Reis
* Sister Suzanne Homeyer
* Sister Mary Virginia Schmidt
* Sister Karen Mohan
* Sister Katherine Mullin
* Sister Brenda Lisenby

Many of The Sisters were in the audience at an event where Mary was speaking about her mission of forgiveness and how she forgave the man who shot and killed her only child at a house party in 1993.

Moved by Mary's presentation, several of The Sisters went up to Mary to introduce themselves and express their appreciation for her story. The Sisters invited Mary to their next community meeting to meet other Sisters in the monastery and share more of her story. A connection was born. The Sisters embraced Mary and made her a part of their Catholic family.

What an interesting collaboration! A group of white nuns opening their arms to an African-American woman who inspired them with a rare form of forgiveness.

With The Sisters' help, Mary's organization, From Death To Life, began to grow. Mary had started From Death To Life a few years earlier as a support group for mothers like herself who had lost children to violence. Mary's connection with The Sisters organization led to more speaking engagements and appearances. But The Sisters realized something was missing.

Whenever Mary made appearances, she didn't have much material to leave with the people who heard her speak. The Sisters believed Mary should have a more definitive, detailed portrayal of her story. Several years go by before one of The Sisters has a chance encounter with a retired sportswriter.

After working 34 years as a sportswriter for newspapers in Chicago, Phoenix and Minneapolis-

St. Paul, I decided to hang up all my press passes to do more work in the community. I got a chance to work with The Visitation Sisters on a National Night Out event in the summer of 2015. Sister Mary Frances knew I was a former journalist and must have made a mental note during the event.

A few months later, Sister Mary Frances gives me a call to tell me about a lady named "Mary Johnson" and wants to know if I would be interested in writing her story.

One thing led to another, and here we are.

As a sportswriter who covered the NBA, NFL, major-league baseball, college basketball and boxing, I can say I came across some interesting characters and unique individuals. But I had never sat at a table with a convicted murderer. A vital part in researching this story was getting to know Oshea Israel.

Oshea was 16 when he fatally shot Mary's son, Laramiun Byrd, at a house party. At the time, Oshea was known as Marlon Green, his given birth name.

When I met Oshea, he had been out of prison for six years but he was still on probation. His probation ended on Aug. 18, 2018.

Before we did any interviews, I spent a few days with Oshea, so we could establish a comfort zone. We talked a lot about our common interests, particularly music. I love my R&B old-school; he loves his rap and hip-hop. Music became an icebreaker for us, as well as the subject of our hometown. We both grew up on Chicago's South Side. Oshea was born in 1976, the same year my oldest son, Shandel, came into this world.

Oshea and I had a lot of conversation pieces, which helped us establish mutual respect. I felt I could challenge him when necessary to get the information I needed.

Without that bond, I'm not sure how cooperative and enlightening Oshea would have been throughout this process. He was magnificent at every turn.

Leading into our fourth interview session, I told Oshea this is the day where we talk about The Party. "We're going to have to go down that road today… I know it might be uncomfortable for you."

Without hesitation, he responded: "I'm ready."

On a balmy summer afternoon in a North Minneapolis restaurant, Oshea and I talk for 90 minutes about the events leading up to the party and what happened there.

I'm drilling him with questions to get every possible detail I can, and he's cooperating.

Oshea essentially gives me a play-by-play account. But as we get closer to the shooting, he becomes more agitated with my questions.

The look in his eyes tells me this trip down memory lane is bothering him, as if he's in that house again.

"You're just determined to get all this out of me aren't you?"

Without hesitation, I said, "Yep!"

After expressing his frustration with my questions, he provides a few more dramatic details of his confrontation with Laramiun. What happens next shakes me.

Oshea looks directly in my eyes and firmly says, "…Then I raised the gun and I shot him."

Hands down, that's the most powerful quote ever given to me in my entire career as a journalist.

While working on this project, I had the privilege of getting to know Oshea and Mary and chronicle the inspiring transformation in their lives — from tragedy to hatred… to forgiveness.

The unfolding of this story is truly "Beyond Belief."

# Two Mothers

Long time ago, so I have been told,

Two angels once met on streets paved with gold.

"By the stars in your crown," said the one to the other, "I see that on earth, you too, were a mother."

"And by the blue-tinted halo you wear,

You, too, have known sorrow and deepest despair."

"Ah, yes," she replied. "I once had a son,

A sweet little lad, full of laughter and fun."

"But tell of your child."

"Oh, I knew I was blessed From the moment I first held him close to my breast, And my heart almost burst with the joy of that day."

"Ah, yes," said the other. "I felt the same way."

The former continued, "The first steps he took…So eager and breathless; the sweet startled look Which came over his face…he trusted me so."

"Ah, yes," said the other. "How well do I know."

"But soon he had grown to a tall handsome boy, So stalwart and kind…and it gave me so much joy To have him just walk down the street by my side."

"Ah, yes," said the other mother. "I felt the same pride."

"How often I shielded and spared him from pain And when he for others was so cruelly slain When they crucified him…and they spat in his face How gladly would I have hung there in his place!"

A moment of silence…

"Oh, then you are she The mother of Christ"…And she fell on one knee.

But the blessed one raised her up, drawing her near And kissed from the cheek of the woman, a tear. "Tell me the name of the son you love so, That I may share with your grief and your woe."

She lifted her eyes, looking straight at the other,

"He was Judas Iscariot…I am his mother."

*Author Unknown*

**Ray Richardson**, a native of Chicago's South
Side, was a sportswriter for 34 years.
The Illinois State University graduate wrote for the
Chicago Daily Defender, Phoenix Gazette and St. Paul
Pioneer Press. He has covered the NBA, NFL, Major-
League Baseball, college football, men's and women's
college basketball and professional boxing.
Richardson is an active member of the National
Association of Black Journalists and a founding
member of the NABJ Sports Task Force, a nationwide
group of African-American sportswriters and
sportscasters. Richardson also hosts a popular R&B
oldies show on KMOJ-FM (kmojfm.com) in
Minneapolis-St. Paul.

**E-mail:** rayrich55@gmail.com
**Facebook:** Ray Richardson
**Twitter:** @rayrich55

CPSIA information can be obtained
at www.ICGtesting.com
Printed in the USA
LVHW050314180221
679454LV00039B/452

9 798606 880966